GARDEN TOURING
IN THE PACIFIC NORTHWEST

A GUIDE TO GARDENS AND SPECIALTY NURSERIES IN OREGON, WASHINGTON, AND BRITISH COLUMBIA

JAN KOWALCZEWSKI WHITNER

Alaska Northwest Boo
ANCHORAGE ◆ SEATTLE ◆ PO

D0958394

For Steve, Pam, and Henry
—the road warriors

Library of Congress Cataloging-in-Publication Data
Whitner, Jan Kowalczewski, 1949–
     Garden touring in the Pacific Northwest : a guide to gardens and specialty nurseries in
  Oregon, Washington, and British Columbia / by Jan Kowalczewski Whitner.
        p.   cm.
    Includes index.
    ISBN 0-88240-429-6
    1. Gardens—Northwest, Pacific—Guidebooks.   2. Nurseries (Horticulture)—Northwest,
Pacific—Guidebooks. I. Title.
    SB466.U65N768   1993
    712' .5'09795—dc20   92-39393
                                                     CIP

Project editor, Ellen Harkins Wheat
Editors, Carolyn Smith and Alice Copp Smith
Book and cover design, Alice C. Merrill
Illustrations, David Lund
Maps, David Berger
Cover photo: Ohme Gardens (Dick Busher)

Some material in this book appeared previously in the *Seattle Times* and in *Pacific Northwest* and *Greater Seattle* magazines in similar or identical form.

The illustration on page 131 was drawn from a photograph entitled "The Rose Garden—Summer," supplied by The Butchart Gardens Ltd.

Alaska Northwest Books™
An Imprint of Graphic Arts Center Publishing Company
Editorial Office: 2208 N.W. Market Street, Suite 300
Seattle, WA 98107

Printed on recycled paper in the United States of America

CONTENTS

Acknowledgments

I would like to express thanks to the following individuals who made researching this book a pleasure as well as an education: Hilda Cullen, Alan Houghton, Todd Major, Nancy J. Chapman, Eileen Landergen, Rich Van De Mark, Darlene Strozut, Bill Willard, Margaret Willoughby, Brian Rowbottom, Beth Leader, Carol Burgess, Maureen Beckstead, Don Brooks, Van Bobbitt, Fred Nilsen, Sue Thomas, Claire Met, Heather Day, John Barker, Bill Heubener, Rosemary Wills, Craig Sanders, Patsy Duggan, Valerie Finding, and Joe Mullen.

Special thanks are due to Stephen M. Whitner, a modern Odysseus whose steadfast navigation helped bring this paper vessel safely to harbor.

When April with its showers sweet
The drought of March hath pierced to the root
And bathed every vein in such liquor
Of which virtue engendered is the flower. . . .
Then folks long to go on pilgrimages . . .
For to seek foreign shores in sundry lands.
—Geoffrey Chaucer,
Prologue to *The Canterbury Tales*

INTRODUCTION

It's no accidental link Chaucer establishes between the regeneration of the natural world every spring and the age-old human desire to seek out new places and see new sights.

The same restless seasonal charge that wakes up plants—impelling them to thrust their stalks up through the steaming earth and unfurl leaves along their branches—also impels people to set out on the road to travel.

But sightseers have many reasons to embark on journeys besides the simple atavistic urge to wander. In the Middle Ages, pilgrims visited holy shrines to strengthen their sense of connection to a deeper and more significant world. By the eighteenth century, the leisured classes were sending their sons on grand tours of the Continent's cities, courts, and ancient ruins in order to polish their budding tastes and manners. And today, modern travelers seek out exotic cultures and unspoiled landscapes, eager to explore the world's diversity even while, and probably because, it continues to disappear at a rapid rate.

Garden touring—a special subgenre of sightseeing—is becoming increasingly popular in the United States and Canada, and gardeners frequently play both the pilgrim and the tourist when they visit their nations' public gardens, conservatories, arboreta, and botanical gardens.

On the most significant level, we garden visitors want to find something magical, something that will transform our sense of what a garden is or can be. On a more practical level, we also want to garner snippets of information—the name of a flower, a better way to site a shrub—to help us improve our own gardens. And, of course, many gardeners like to visit a beautifully conceived and executed garden simply to savor its maker's creative response to a specific site and a specific set of growing conditions.

Whatever their reasons for touring a garden, most visitors find it valuable to know something beforehand of the site's purpose and scope so that they can gain a context for understanding what they are about to see. As a longtime resident of and gardener in the Pacific Northwest, I wrote this guidebook to help acquaint readers—both gardeners who live here and visitors to the region—with the history, layout, and plant collections of the Pacific Northwest's major public gardens. In presenting these factual "bones," I hope that something of each garden's atmosphere—even, one might say, of its spirit—shines through as well. While researching the book I discovered public gardens and nurseries previously unknown to me, and I hope that among the 91 public gardens and 56 specialty nurseries listed here readers will find some new favorites too.

GARDEN STYLES IN THE
MARITIME PACIFIC NORTHWEST

Visitors who tour the long corridor of land that stretches between the Pacific Ocean and the Cascade Mountains from southern Oregon to lower British Columbia encounter natural landscapes whose beauty surpasses that of any garden created by human hands.

The region displays an astounding variety of landforms and vegetation: delicate shore flowers digging into sandy ridges at the ocean's edge, rain-drenched firs and mosses blanketing coastal forests, scrubby shrubs fringing rivers that twist through broad glacial valleys, and stony mountain slopes dotted with pines stunted by snow and wind. This natural landscape forms the backdrop—literally and metaphorically—for the region's public gardens, and its wild influence is reflected in the naturalistic designs and informal planting schemes that many of them display.

Along with this naturalistic strand, two other garden styles have twined themselves into our present-day Northwest gardening culture. One, the Japanese, emphasizes informal (but highly sophisticated) planting schemes and the use of evergreens, with their subtle shadings of texture and shape, as the backbone of the garden. This tradition flourishes in its classic form in Portland's Japanese Garden and in the Japanese Garden in Seattle's Washington Park Arboretum. It also flourishes in "hybrid" gardens that have adapted Japanese principles of design to New World scales and New World plant palettes, such as Vancouver's Nitobe

Memorial Garden and Seattle's Kubota Gardens.

The second style, which derives from European—and most especially English—gardening traditions, emphasizes the use of exotic perennials, shrubs, and trees in garden plans that range from the comfortably relaxed to the highly formal. This diverse tradition lives on in the perennial borders found at Salem's Deepwood Estate and Victoria's Government House, in the region's arboreta and botanical gardens, in the colorful annual beds in various municipal parks, and in such multiroomed estate gardens as Portland's Elk Rock and Victoria's Hatley Castle.

Although the natural landscape and the Japanese and European gardening traditions form the roots of the Pacific Northwest garden style, our region is currently evolving its own characteristic garden culture. This culture is being formed in part due to the Pacific Northwest's unique climate, which accommodates the growing requirements of a worldwide range of temperate zone plants, and in part due to the region's role as a cultural crossroads on the Pacific Rim. Such factors predispose the area's gardeners to experiment with a rich variety of plants and design traditions when they design their own gardens. And all these factors, in turn, contribute to making the Pacific Northwest a horticultural hotspot—one whose public gardens reflect the region's general trends toward assimilation and eclecticism.

HOW TO USE THIS BOOK

- Entries are organized geographically, starting with southern Oregon and traveling north to British Columbia; within the environs of major cities, gardens are listed alphabetically. Major garden destinations are treated at length.
- Traveling directions are given, where possible, from the nearest city, freeway, highway, or major thoroughfare. An updated local map is an invaluable tool for the garden visitor; over time, street names may change and new roads may appear, especially in suburban and rural areas.
- Each entry concludes with access information; although this information is accurate at the time of writing, we suggest visitors phone ahead for the most current information on fees, hours, path conditions, and seasonal displays and events.
- Because admission fees change more often than other factors, we categorize admission policy only as "fee," "donation," or "free." Fees can vary widely, from nominal charges under a dollar to more than $10. Please note that donations often play a crucial role in the development and upkeep of public gardens.
- See "Gardens by Type" at the back of the book for a list of gardens grouped by category—Asian Gardens, Estate Gardens, Conservatories, and so on.

- "Regional Specialty Nurseries" with display gardens are listed at the back of the book.
- At the back, "Private Garden Tours" lists regional organizations that sponsor tours of private gardens.
- The glossary defines some gardening terms that readers may find unfamiliar.
- The index presents the gardens and nurseries alphabetically.
- "Garden Notes" offers blank pages for note-taking.

KEY TO GARDEN TYPES

The symbols below indicate the major garden types found in this book. They appear at the beginning of each entry and allow you to find the garden types featured at a glance. Many gardens fall into more than one category; see Gardens by Type at the back of the book for other categories, including Child-Friendly Gardens, Gardens Available for Private Functions, Gardens for Picnicking, and Gardens of Winter Interest.

 Arboreta and Gardens with Notable Tree Collections

 Native Plant Collections

 Asian Gardens

 Natural Areas

 Botanical Gardens

 Rhododendron Gardens

 Conservatories

 Rose Gardens

 Display, Demonstration, and Estate Gardens

OREGON

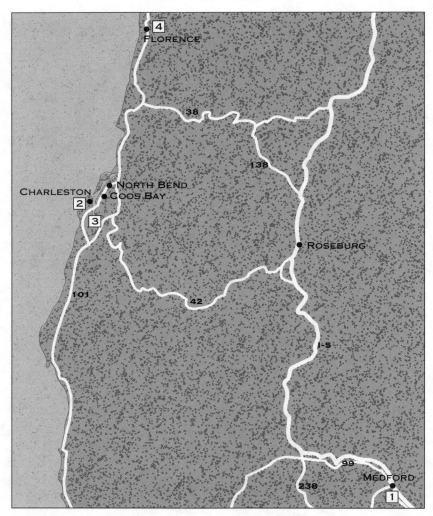

1. Jackson & Perkins Test and Display Garden, *Medford*
2. Shore Acres State Park Botanical Garden, *Coos Bay*
3. South Slough Estuarine Reserve, *Charleston*
4. Darlingtonia Botanical Wayside, *Florence*

Shore Acres State Park Botanical Garden, *Coos Bay*

SOUTHERN OREGON

Jackson & Perkins Test and Display Garden

MEDFORD

Established in 1971 by Jackson and Perkins, one of the country's leading developers and marketers of hybrid roses, this 1-acre site is wedged between Highway 99 and a multistoried business building. Laid out like a Rose Hall of Fame, the garden features displays of golden oldies—best-selling hybrids developed by Jackson & Perkins in the past—and testing beds for the up-and-coming stars—candidates being evaluated for future marketing.

Visitors can play their part in determining which roses appear in American gardens in coming years by stopping at the octagonal visitor's center to vote for the hybrids they find most appealing. They can also snap their catalog favorites in the "photography beds" and peruse a bed of miniatures and standards. The roses reach their peak in June and July.

2836 S Pacific Hwy (old Hwy 99), Medford OR 97501, (503) 776-2277. Daily during daylight hours. Roses bloom June–Sept; call ahead for best viewing time. From Medford, take S Pacific Hwy (old Hwy 99) just south of the city limits and watch for signs.

Labels; self-guiding brochures; guided tours for groups of 10 or more with 48 hours notice; visitors' center; restrooms; wheelchair-accessible; free.

Shore Acres State Park Botanical Garden
COOS BAY

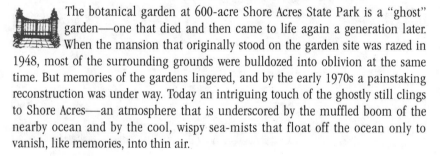 The botanical garden at 600-acre Shore Acres State Park is a "ghost" garden—one that died and then came to life again a generation later. When the mansion that originally stood on the garden site was razed in 1948, most of the surrounding grounds were bulldozed into oblivion at the same time. But memories of the gardens lingered, and by the early 1970s a painstaking reconstruction was under way. Today an intriguing touch of the ghostly still clings to Shore Acres—an atmosphere that is underscored by the muffled boom of the nearby ocean and by the cool, wispy sea-mists that float off the ocean only to vanish, like memories, into thin air.

SIGNIFICANT FEATURES
- a formal garden, a Japanese pond garden, and a rose garden
- trails leading through Northwest forest plantings to views of the magnificent southern Oregon seacoast

HISTORY
The gardens at Shore Acres were established in 1906, when lumber magnate Louis J. Simpson began building a splendid 3-story mansion overlooking the Pacific Ocean near Cape Arago in southwestern Oregon. During its heyday, five gardeners tended the estate's extensive grounds, which featured exotic plants brought from all corners of the earth by Simpson's fleet of sailing ships.

Fires destroyed the first Simpson mansion in 1921 and parts of the garden in 1937. The mansion and gardens were rebuilt, but by the late 1930s the timber industry was in a period of decline, and Mr. Simpson found it too expensive to continue to maintain the estate. The Oregon State Parks Division purchased the estate in 1942 and six years later tore down the mansion, which had fallen into complete disrepair; at the same time bull-dozers filled in the ponds and planting beds in the gardens.

The gardens remained derelict until 1971, when the state parks staff began interviewing Simpson family members and researching old plans and photographs with the aim of restoring the grounds as accurately as possible. By 1975 the renovation was complete, and today visitors can view the gardens in much of their former glory.

THE GARDEN PLAN

An entry gate leads visitors directly into the garden's largest and most formal room, where square and rectangular parterres bordered in boxwood contain flowering shrubs, annuals, and perennials. Simpson elected to plant his formal garden in a sheltered area without a distracting ocean view, and its clipped precision contrasts with the shaggy informality of the surrounding forest's Sitka spruces, Douglas firs, and Monterey cypresses.

At the farther end of the formal garden, stone steps lead down to an expansive water-lily pond. The garden room that circles the pond blends Japanese and romantic touches, including stone lanterns and a pair of blue herons made of copper whose reflections ripple on the water's surface.

Beyond the water-lily pond lie trails that take visitors first to a small rose garden and then on to a cliffside stroll along the Pacific Ocean. An enclosed viewing area atop one of the cliffs marks where the Simpson mansions originally stood.

BEST TIMES TO VIEW

In spring, blooming rhododendrons, azaleas, and iris fringe the water-lily pond; roses, dahlias, hydrangeas, and a host of perennials and annuals flower all summer in the formal garden. Walks along the ocean are a treat at any time of year, but they are most dramatic during the winter.

13030 Cape Arago Hwy, P.O. Box 1172, Coos Bay, OR 97420, (503) 888-3732. Daily during daylight hours. From Coos Bay, follow Hwy 14 approximately 12 miles southwest to Sunset Bay, then follow signs.

Brochures; visitors' center; gift shop; restrooms; some wheelchair access; free (small parking fee in summer).

South Slough Estuarine Reserve

CHARLESTON

 This 4400-acre plant and wildlife sanctuary has a 1½-mile trail along which visitors can see how habitats characteristic of the coast—forest, streamside, estuary, and shoreline—interrelate.

P.O. Box 5417, Charleston, OR 97420, (503) 888-5558. Daily during daylight hours (visitors' center open daily June–Aug, 8:30–4:30, weekdays, Sept–May, 8:30–4:30). From Charleston, drive south on Seven Dials Rd for about 4 miles and watch for signs to the reserve.
   Brochures; tours; visitors' center; programs; restrooms; free.

Darlingtonia Botanical Wayside

FLORENCE

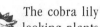 The cobra lily (*Darlingtonia californica*) is one of those sinister-looking plants that might seem more at home in a steamy tropical swamp than in the coastal forests of northern California and southwestern Oregon. Yet clumps of these insect-eating perennials inhabit the region's bogs in altitudes between sea level and 6000 feet. Insects attracted by the sweet nectar of the *Darlingtonia* crawl down its slippery insides, falling into a pool of liquid containing bacteria that break them down into food. The plant's waxy leaves swell into flecked and spotted tubes, making its colonies look like hooded cobras massed in a boggy nest.

Visitors can easily view a patch of these botanical curiosities in their native habitat from a short, signed trail at the wayside. The plants are visible any time between March and September, but their purple flowers, shooting 3 or 4 feet high on slender stalks, bloom only in April, May, and June. Try to visit early in the day, before traffic on the nearby highway cuts into the spooky charm the cobra lilies cast.

Daily, dawn to dusk. From Florence, drive 5 miles north on U.S. Hwy 101 and follow signs.
   Some labels; restrooms; free.

Deepwood Gardens, *Salem*

CENTRAL OREGON
George Owen Memorial Rose Garden
EUGENE

 Trellises supporting old-fashioned climbing roses pruned into hearts and fans form the backdrop to this 5-acre All-America Selections rose garden on the banks of the Willamette River. Island beds containing some 100 varieties of labeled hybrid teas and floribundas surround empress trees (*Paulownia tomentosa*), silk trees (*Albizia julibrissin*), magnolias, conifers, and a stately old cherry tree that was planted in the 1860s. The roses bloom most profusely in mid-June. The garden, which was established in 1951, is maintained by the Eugene Parks and Recreation Department with the assistance of the Eugene Rose Society.

On N Jefferson St at the river's edge. Mailing address: Parks Services Division,

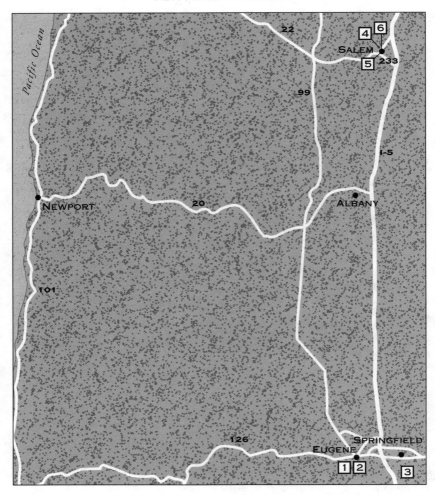

1. George Owen Memorial Rose Garden, *Eugene*
2. Hendricks Park Rhododendron Garden, *Eugene*
3. Mount Pisgah Arboretum, *Eugene*
4. Bush's Pasture Park, *Salem*
5. Deepwood Gardens, *Salem*
6. Willamette University Campus, *Salem*

210 Cheshire St, Eugene, OR 97401, (503) 687-5333. Daily during daylight hours. From downtown Eugene, drive north on Washington St; turn left on 1st Ave and then right on Jefferson St.

Brochure; picnic tables; restrooms; some wheelchair access; free.

Hendricks Park Rhododendron Garden
EUGENE

 Handsome stone garden structures, a setting suffused with the Pacific Northwest's famous pearly light, and native trees and shrubs arranged at their most ornamental all contribute to make this spot Eugene's prettiest, as well as its oldest, park.

Although the park itself was established in 1906, it wasn't until 1951 that the Rhododendron Garden—a 10-acre installation within the larger park—was planted through the efforts of the local chapter of the American Rhododendron Society. Because society members donated cuttings of their own, some rare species and hybrids are represented in the 5000 varieties of rhododendrons and azaleas that make up the collection. Interplanted among them are magnolias, dogwoods, viburnums, and witch hazels. Blooms are at their peak in April and May.

Summit Ave and Skyline Dr. Mailing address: Parks Services Division, 210 Cheshire St, Eugene, OR 97401, (503) 687-5333. Daily, dawn to dusk. From Hwy 99-126 (also called W Franklin Blvd), turn south onto Walnut St and then turn east onto Summit Ave.

Some labels; maps and plant identifiers (intermittently) available at a box near main entry; guided tours (call Eugene Parks and Recreation Dept); restrooms; wheelchair-accessible; free.

Mount Pisgah Arboretum
EUGENE

 This 120-acre sanctuary for native and exotic plants, named for the mountain from which Moses first saw the Promised Land, has trails that loop through several habitats characteristic of the area, including marshes, wildflower meadows, river banks, and forested hillsides. A series of international groves that will feature trees native to diverse temperate zones, such as regions of Chile, China, and Tasmania, are being planted by the volunteer Friends of Mount Pisgah Arboretum, a group that developed and now maintains the arboretum.

Southeast of Eugene in Howard Buford Recreation Area. Mailing address: Friends of Mount Pisgah Arboretum, P.O. Box 5621, Eugene OR 97405, (503) 747-3817. Daily during daylight hours. From Eugene, take I-5 south to 30th Ave exit, travel east on Seavey Loop, and follow signs.

Self-guiding brochures; workshops, children's programs, seasonal festivals; picnic area; restrooms; limited wheelchair access; free.

Bush's Pasture Park
SALEM

 Located just down Mission Street from Deepwood Gardens (see next entry), this park originally formed the grounds of a fine old pioneer home built in 1877 by a prominent Salemite, Asahel Bush; some ancient fruit and shade trees planted at that time still cluster near the restored house. Today, Bush's Pasture Park is administered by the Salem Parks and Recreation Agency, with the assistance of the nonprofit Friends of Bush Gardens.

The park features an extensive rose garden, with regimented rows of labeled hybrid teas, floribundas, and grandifloras alternating with old-fashioned climbers on trellises. Many are varieties that were brought west by pioneers before the turn of the century—their common names of the period are preserved on the labels, along with their botanical names. A brochure listing rose varieties and their locations in the planting beds is available at Bush House (where you also can visit the region's oldest conservatory: weekdays, year-round 9–4; weekends, June through August, 12–5; September through May, 2–5.) Browse and sniff your way through the rose garden in early June, when it is especially floriferous and odiferous.

600 Mission St SE, Salem OR 97302, (503) 363-4714. Daily, dawn to dusk. From I-5, take exit 253 onto the Mission St overpass. Travel on Mission St one block; look for signs to the park on the left side of the street.

Brochures; programs; restrooms; some wheelchair access; free.

Deepwood Gardens
SALEM

A sophisticated layout and elegant hardscapes distinguish the multi-leveled, multiroomed gardens of the Deepwood Estate. Designed in 1929 by the noted Pacific Northwest landscape architects Elizabeth Lord and Edith Schryver, Deepwood Gardens features painted lattice fences and arbors, an ornate wrought-iron pergola, clipped boxwood hedges, and lush plantings edged with precise borders, resulting in a garden design that is formal yet inviting, delicate and yet "done."

Lord and Schryver's achievement at Deepwood is especially noteworthy because the garden is small (less than 2 acres) and because it is on a difficult site—its topography prevents a natural interface between the house and grounds. Despite these challenges, the garden features a spacious design that feels comfortably integrated with the house. Lord and Schryver also used a choice selection of plants at Deepwood; today the gardens feature flower borders filled with unusual perennials as well as beautifully textured and shaded plantings of trees and shrubs.

SIGNIFICANT FEATURES
- the only garden designed by Northwest landscape architects Lord and Schryver currently open to the public
- an exquisite design skillfully combining formal and informal garden areas
- sumptuous perennial borders
- on the National Register of Historic Places

HISTORY
Deepwood House itself was built in 1894 in the picturesque Queen Anne style popular in late 19th-century Salem; the lawn and shrubs at the front of the house date from that period. The gardens at the sides and back of the house, now termed Deepwood Gardens proper, weren't begun until 1929, when the owner of Deepwood, Alice Brown Powell, commissioned her friends Lord and Schryver to create a place with "some final little charm of its own that any garden must have in order to really live."

Both Elizabeth Lord, an Oregon native, and Edith Schryver had received their professional training as landscape architects at Lowthorpe School of Landscape Architecture for Women in Groton, Massachusetts, one of the few landscape architecture programs available to women in the 1920s. Finding a commonality in their approach to garden design, the two decided to practice their profession as partners in Salem. During the next four decades, the partners created private gardens in Seattle, Tacoma, Portland, and Salem, with Schryver planning the overall design and Lord handling the plantings. Deepwood, one of their early commissions, represents the period when they were first learning how to integrate the contemporary European principles of garden design they admired with plants common to North American gardens.

Sometime in the 1930s, when the garden had become well established, Alice Brown Powell wrote to Lord and Schryver: "You've made it beautifully. . . . I'll never be satisfied just to have it please one's eye—it must stir the imagination—or it's no real garden." According to Powell's own standard, Deepwood is indeed a real garden.

In 1968 the estate was purchased by the city of Salem. A nonprofit corporation, The Friends of Deepwood, now maintains it with the assistance of a volunteer organization called the Deepwood Gardeners. Before her death in 1984, Edith Schryver advised the Gardeners on Deepwood's full restoration.

THE GARDEN PLAN

Deepwood has several major garden rooms that are linked by paths, flights of steps, arbors, and evergreen hedges. Visitors can enter the garden from the parking area on the northwest corner of the site, but since this entry plunges quickly into one of the more complex garden areas, it may prove more interesting to approach Deepwood from the front, via the lawn and path on the west side of the house.

Taking this route, one first encounters the **Great Room,** a formal lawn bordered by clipped boxwoods and holly hedges, some of them ingeniously foreshortened to create a sense of depth along the north–south axis. At the north end of the Great Room is a delicate, turn-of-the-century wrought-iron gazebo that sets off the formal greenery surrounding it.

Taking the path to the right of the gazebo, one walks under ivy-covered trellises into the **Chinese Garden,** a small, rectangular room with clipped boxwood hedges arranged like scrolls along its wrought-iron fences. At the far end is a small centerpiece of clipped hedges that once served as the base of a large, ornate Oriental jar. The jar has since vanished, and the area would benefit by the installation of a similarly imaginative focal point.

Continuing south in the general direction of the house, one follows the side path that curves downhill on the east side of the house toward the **Secret Garden,** a romantic hollow designed by Alice Brown Powell that features informal plantings (many of them native), a small pond, and a broken stone column half buried in groundcovers and shrubs.

Retracing their path around the back of the house and walking west, past the entry to the Great Room, visitors encounter the carriage house. A long path to the right of the carriage house leads them to the most complex area in the gardens: the **Moon Garden,** with its teahouse, surrounded by lattice fences that are painted in Lord and Schryver's trademark gray-green. The flower borders in this area are both formal and elegant. In early summer drifts of foxgloves, alyssum, late peonies, and poppies ring all the changes on creams, pinks, and lavenders.

Outside the garden's west boundary stands a long, deep, sumptuous herbaceous border designed according to the influential British designer Gertrude Jekyll's principles of color progression—starting at one end of the border with cool lavenders, creams, and pinks, then moving toward deep, warm golds and scarlets in the center and back again to pastels at the other end. Growing more opulent and sophisticated each year under the care of the Deepwood Gardeners, this border acts as a stunning finale to an altogether delicious garden.

Behind the Deepwood greenhouse runs the **Ruth Steiner Fry Nature Trail,** along which visitors will find signs for native trees. Braille signs also are present. Wildflowers bloom along the trail in March and April.

BEST TIMES TO VIEW

The garden is given structure year-round by hedges of boxwood, yew, laurel, and holly; spring's cherries, crabapples, magnolias, and azaleas give way to a profusion of flowering herbaceous perennials, clematis, and roses during summer. In fall, anemones, aconitum, and turning leaves glow against the evergreen background.

1116 Mission St SE, Salem, OR 97302, (503) 363-1825. Garden: Sun–Fri, dawn to dusk. (Deepwood House is open May–Sept, Sun–Fri, noon–4:30; call for winter hours. A small admission fee is charged to tour the house.) From I-5, take exit 253 onto Mission St overpass and continue to the corner of Mission and 12th.

Brochure; programs; restrooms; some wheelchair access; free.

Willamette University Campus
SALEM

This pretty campus, located several blocks north of Bush's Pasture Park, is crisscrossed by streams and picturesque ravines. Mill Race Park, a 4-block enclave on campus between Pringle and Church streets, features waterstairs, plazas, small ponds, and a stream fringed by native trees and groundcovers, some of which are labeled.

Mission St and 12th St; no phone. Daily during daylight hours. From I-5 south of Salem, take exit 253, travel west on Mission St, and follow signs for 12th St/Willamette University.

Campus restrooms; some wheelchair access; free.

PORTLAND AND ENVIRONS, OREGON

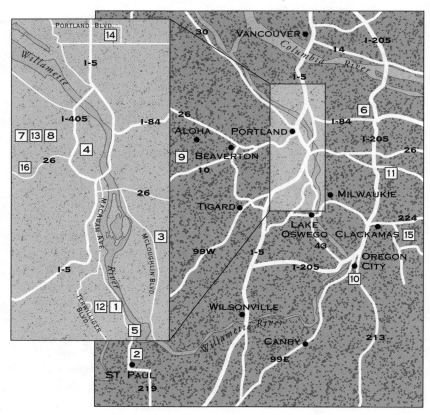

1. Berry Botanic Garden, *Portland*
2. Cecil and Molly Smith Rhododendron Garden, *St. Paul*
3. Crystal Springs Rhododendron Garden, *Portland*
4. Downtown Parks and Squares, *Portland*
5. Elk Rock, the Garden of the Bishop's Close, *Portland*
6. The Grotto, *Portland*
7. Hoyt Arboretum, *Portland*
8. International Rose Test Garden, *Portland*
9. Jenkins Estate, *Aloha*
10. John Inskeep Environmental Learning Center, *Oregon City*
11. Leach Botanical Garden, *Portland*
12. Lewis and Clark College Campus, *Portland*
13. Portland Japanese Garden, *Portland*
14. Sunken Rose Garden at Peninsula Park, *Portland*
15. Tallina's Garden, *Clackamas*
16. Washington Park Zoo Grounds, *Portland*

Elk Rock, the Garden of the Bishop's Close, *Portland*

PORTLAND AND ENVIRONS

Berry Botanic Garden

PORTLAND

Plant collectors are an unusual variety of the genus *Gardener.* Most gardeners admire plants that are beautiful, tasty, or useful, but collectors reserve their special adoration for those plants that are rare.

The Pacific Northwest has had its share of avid plant collectors, beginning with early European explorers such as the Scotsman David Douglas (the ubiquitous Douglas fir is named in his honor), who scoured Northwest forests for new plants to take back to the Old World. Today Northwest plant enthusiasts reverse the process, bringing home to our region seeds or cuttings of unusual plants—ferns from the tropical jungles of Central America or dwarf rhododendrons native to the Himalayas—which they collect abroad.

Berry Botanic Garden, established in 1938, originally was the private garden of a dedicated Northwest collector, Rae Selling Berry, who spent a considerable number of her 95 years (1881–1976) in acquiring and propagating species plants from around the world. Today visitors strolling the garden's six acres of woods, rock gardens, and collection display areas can enjoy the fruits of Mrs. Berry's lifelong devotion to unusual and rare plants.

SIGNIFICANT FEATURES

- extensive collections of species rhododendrons, primulas, lilies, alpines, and Pacific Northwest native plants
- a participating institution of the National Center for Plant Conservation
- on-site library and herbarium

HISTORY

Rae Selling Berry acquired the site of the present garden because her plant collections had outgrown a previous home and she wanted to continue expanding them while also providing them with optimal growing conditions. After considering a number of properties that had the varied soil types, exposures, and topography the collections required, she ultimately decided on the present site because it possessed a special woodland beauty in addition to all of the other features. In the years that followed, Mrs. Berry continued to develop her collections with an eye to their ornamental potential and with an appreciation of the natural setting surrounding them. The result is a garden that general visitors can enjoy as much as do specialty plant devotees.

In the 40 years during which it remained her private garden, Mrs. Berry grew plants from seeds and cuttings she collected on trips through the western United States and Alaska; she also imported seeds from Asia, South America, and the Near East. Due to her exceptional gardening skills, many varieties of wild species plants previously uncultivated have flourished and reproduced in the garden.

After Mrs. Berry died in 1976, her garden almost was lost to developers, who wanted to subdivide the property into residential lots. By 1978 a new nonprofit organization, the Friends of Rae Selling Berry, had raised sufficient funds to purchase the garden and open it to the public. Today the garden displays rare species plants, conducts botanical research, and maintains the Seed Bank for Rare and Endangered Species of the Pacific Northwest.

THE GARDEN PLAN

Berry Botanic Garden has developed a variety of microclimates to accommodate its large range of native and exotic plants. Woodland areas with dappled shade feature over 1000 species rhododendrons, many of them native to Asia, including *Rhododendron decorum* and *R. calophytum,* as well as Pacific Northwest native groundcovers such as redwood sorrel fairy bells (*Disporum hookeri*), wild ginger (*Asarum*), *Vancouveria hexandra,* and vanilla leaf (*Achlys triphylla*). A bog area supports colonies of cobra lily (*Darlingtonia californica*), sundew (*Drosera*), and butterwort (*Pingguicula*), along with bog orchids (*Habenaria*), monkey flower (*Mimulus*), swamp cranberry (*Vaccinium oxycoccos*), and lady's slipper (*Cypripedium*). An open, sunny rock garden behind the house displays over 600 alpine species, mostly native to the Pacific Rim, in rocky outcroppings and troughs, and meadows feature over half of the world's 100 lily species interplanted with annual wildflowers. One hundred species of primulas, described as Mrs. Berry's special love, inhabit damp areas in the garden, with candelabra primroses especially thick above the lawn near the house.

BEST TIMES TO VIEW

In winter, *Viburnum grandiflorum, V. farreri,* and *V.* x *bodnantense* bloom, as do Chinese witch hazel (*Hamamelis mollis*) and *Rhododendron rubiginosum.* In spring flowering bulbs, various primulas and alpines, a *Magnolia kobus* var. *borealis,* and many of the species rhododendrons flower; wildflowers and candelabra primroses take over in early summer.

11505 SW Summerville Ave, Portland OR 97219, (503) 636-4112. Year-round, Mon–Sat 10–4, by appointment only. Directions are given at time appointment is made.

Labels; brochure; guided tours by arrangement; programs and classes (phone for information); restrooms; limited wheelchair access; fee.

Cecil and Molly Smith
Rhododendron Garden
ST. PAUL

 Asian gardeners call rhododendron blossoms "cloud flowers," a name that seems especially apt in this 5½-acre garden, where towering rhododendrons rear into the mist, their blooms hanging over visitors' heads like dewy jewels.

Cecil Smith began the garden in 1951 by incorporating rhododendrons, many of them species types grown from seed collected in the Himalayas and other exotic locales, into an already existing woodland setting—a gently sloping hillside looking over a quiet rural valley. Today, 40 years on, 400 species and hybrid rhododendrons weave together with native firs, paperbark maples (*Acer griseum*), evergreen and deciduous huckleberries (*Vaccinium ovatum* and *V. parvifolium*), Japanese flowering cherries (*Prunus* 'Tai-haku'), and wild hazelnut bushes (*Corylus cornuta*) to make a forest canopy of unusual delicacy.

Planted around the feet of the rhododendrons is a constellation of forest wildflowers and groundcovers, including 13 varieties of trillium, pink dogtooth violets (*Erythronium revoltum*), anemones, cyclamens, bloodroot (*Sanguinaria canadensis*), wild gingers, salal (*Gaultheria shallon*), and various ferns.

Moss-covered stumps and rustic benches add to the charm of this tranquil, artfully designed woodland garden.

Smith also became a hybridizer of international note, and some of his introductions, such as 'Noyo Chief' and 'Cinnamon Bear,' can be seen planted around the grounds. In 1984, after his death, the Portland chapter of the American Rhododendron Society purchased the garden; volunteers from local chapters maintain the garden, continue to collect pollen and to hybridize, and hold open days and plant sales for the public.

5065 Ray Bell Rd, St. Paul, OR 97137; no phone at garden. Open house third Sat in Mar and first and third Sats in April and May, 10–4; other times by arrangement. Contact Portland Chapter, American Rhododendron Society, P.O. Box 86424, Portland, OR 97286-0424, (503) 771-8386. From Portland, take 99W (Pacific Hwy) south to Newberg; turn left on Springbrook Rd, travel about 1 mile, jog right and then left onto Hwy 219 toward St. Paul; cross Willamette River and turn right onto Champoeg Rd; in about 200 yards, where Champoeg Rd turns, drive straight ahead onto Ray Bell Rd.
Restroom; fee.

Crystal Springs Rhododendron Garden
PORTLAND

An airy 7-acre site bordered by ponds and the limpid waters of Crystal Springs Lake, this display garden features hybrid and species rhododendrons interplanted with azaleas, Japanese maples, dogwoods, magnolias, dove trees (*Davidia involucrata*), ferns, and woodland groundcovers. Established in 1950 as a joint venture of the Portland chapter of the American Rhododendron Society and the city of Portland, the garden has recently been renovated with a new waterfall complex and a wide wooden bridge constructed near the entry. Rhododendrons and azaleas reach their peak of bloom in April and May.

Corner of Woodstock and SE 28th Ave, Portland. Mailing address: Portland Park Bureau, 1120 SW 5th Ave, Portland, OR 97204, (503) 771-8386. Daily during daylight hours. From downtown Portland, take Ross Island Bridge to Powell Blvd; travel east on Powell, turn right onto 39th Ave and continue to Woodstock; turn right to 28th.

Brochure; guided tours (call (503) 771-8386 or (503) 796-5193 for info); restrooms; wheelchair-accessible throughout; free.

Downtown Parks and Squares
PORTLAND

Downtown Portland is blessed with a series of squares, parks, and plazas that make strolling along its streets and boulevards an unusually relaxing and rewarding experience. The following spots are well worth visiting:

- **Chapman and Lownsdale squares** are located at the intersection of Main Street and 4th Avenue. Set aside in 1852 for public use, they feature dignified planting schemes and bronze and stone statuary that hearken back to the city's late-Victorian roots.

- **Ira C. Keller Fountain, Lovejoy Fountain,** and **Pettygrove Park** are located in a three-block stretch between 3rd and 2nd avenues, and Harrison and Clay streets. All three were designed by the innovative landscape architecture firm of Halprin and Associates during the 1970s to reflect an appreciation of the Pacific Northwest's natural landscape; Lovejoy and Ira C. Kellar fountains use waterchutes and cascades to transport visitors into an elemental world of rushing, swirling waters; Pettygrove Park lightens the visual weight of the surrounding cityscape with a lacy planting scheme mainly composed of small trees.

- The **South Park Blocks,** between Jackson and Salmon streets off 9th Avenue offer 12 continuous urban squares of mature trees, lawns, and shrubs, allowing visitors to experience open skies, rustling leaves, and green vistas on a spacious scale right in the heart of the city.

Elk Rock, the Garden of the Bishop's Close

PORTLAND

 Structure, pattern, line, and texture—these are the qualities in which well-designed gardens approaching their maturity excel. The heady pleasures of rampant growth and exuberant color that characterize a young garden often give way, as the garden grows older, to a more sober celebration of plant architecture and of the interplay between space, light, and form. As a result, the "ripe" garden offers visitors an atmosphere of tranquility, restraint, and understated elegance. Elk Rock, which ranks among the best of the Pacific Northwest's mature gardens, displays its mellow charms in a natural setting on a rocky ledge high above the Willamette River.

SIGNIFICANT FEATURES

- ◆ a choice selection of exotics that complement their setting among Pacific Northwest natives
- ◆ a fine balance achieved between design considerations and plant displays
- ◆ one of the most extensive collections of magnolias in the Pacific Northwest

HISTORY

Peter Kerr, the original owner of Elk Rock, emigrated from Scotland to Portland in 1888. During the next 18 years he established a grain-exporting business while renting a farm called Cliff Cottage in Dunthorpe, an exclusive Portland neighborhood sited on a cliff overlooking the Willamette River. By 1905 Kerr's business had prospered enough to permit him to purchase the 13-acre farm and to commission the building of a "baronial mansion" on it. While plans for the house were being developed, Kerr engaged John Charles Olmsted, the senior partner in America's most influential landscape architecture firm, the Olmsted Brothers (which had earlier designed park systems for Seattle, Tacoma, and Spokane, as well as New York's Central Park), to design the garden.

For the next ten years Kerr and Olmsted worked to create a garden whose spirit would reflect Kerr's own background and tastes. Broad views over sweeping lawns and an extensive area of clipped boxwood parterres recalled the atmosphere of formal European gardens; the eclectic palette of plants— including many Pacific Northwest natives—and such amenities for outdoor living as a swimming pool, tennis courts, and a nine-hole golf course, fixed the garden firmly in its New World setting. (The swimming pool, tennis courts, and golf course no longer exist.)

Kerr continued to develop his garden for over 60 years, collecting many unusual varieties of magnolias, rhododendrons, and camellias in the process. When he died in 1957 at the age of 95, Kerr's family gave Elk Rock to the Episcopal Diocese of Oregon. The family also gave the diocese an endowment for the upkeep of the garden, which now is maintained, in impeccable style, by a single groundskeeper.

THE GARDEN PLAN

When Olmsted and Kerr began work on Elk Rock, they were dealing with a site already blessed with spectacular views, natural springs, and a profusion of native Douglas firs (*Pseudotsuga menziesii*), western dogwoods (*Cornus nuttallii*), and madrone (*Arbutus menziesii*). The original site was limited, however, by numerous basalt outcroppings, thin soils, and a sometimes treacherous climate featuring mild winters punctuated by occasional devastating cold snaps.

Over the years tons of rock were blasted away, rich soils were brought in, springs were diverted into streams and ponds, and a choice variety of relatively tender exotics were introduced to sheltered spots in the garden. Some rocky outcroppings on steep slopes covered in native shrubs and groundcovers were left unchanged except for the addition of ornamental wildflowers. Thus the garden evolved through a judicious process of altering the natural conditions when necessary and working with them where possible.

Olmsted elected to site the house in a broad hollow well away from the cliff and its views; the expansive lawns that sweep around the house are bordered by evergreen plantings of conifers, rhododendrons, and madrone that serve as backdrops to complementary deciduous trees and shrubs, among them pink dogwood (*Cornus florida* 'Rubra'), flowering cherry (*Prunus serrulata* 'Shirotae'), and many varieties of magnolias. At the back of the house, the lawn rolls up to a broad terrace where such unusual and ornamental trees as *Parrotia persica* and a dove tree (*Davidia involucrata*) are set off by the equally rare shrub *Stachyurus praecox,* whose drooping applegreen and pale-gold flowers open in late winter.

On the fringes of this core lawn are several more intimate garden areas, most of them located on hilly or rocky terrain.

The upper terrace, next to the parking lot, features rubble walls, crisp gravel paths, and trim hedges of boxwood (*Buxus sempervirens*) and Irish yew (*Taxus baccata*) enclosing unusual varieties of witch hazels, including *Hamamelis* x *intermedia* 'Celina' and *H.* x *inter.* 'Ruby Glow.''

Below the upper terrace, a woodsy path lined by iris, ferns, Japanese maples, and rhododendrons leads past a water-lily pool toward the wild part of the garden, a hillside of native trees, shrubs, and groundcovers that looks out over the Willamette River and snow-covered Mount Hood.

Whether viewing the lawn areas, the formal upper terrace, or the informal garden rooms bordering both, visitors may well be struck by the strong architectural bones of this garden's design, as well as by its abundant assortment of unusual plants. This intelligent balance between design considerations and the display of specimen plants, so difficult to achieve and yet so crucial a component of the first-rate garden, is an outstanding feature of Elk Rock. The garden also stands as a model for the integration of carefully selected exotics with native trees and shrubs.

BEST TIMES TO VIEW

Elk Rock offers visual pleasures at any time of the year, but April and May find the garden at its most colorful, with magnolias, dogwoods, rhododendrons, and azaleas in full bloom. Peonies, iris, and a splendid *Wisteria japonica* on the trellis near the parking lot flower in late spring; summer features lilies and a small drought-tolerant garden of herbs and groundcovers called the Chapel Garden. In fall viburnums, katsura trees (*Cercidiphyllum japonicum*), Japanese maples (*Acer japonicum*), and native vine maples (*Acer circinatum*) flare up; plants with winter blooms include sarcococcas, witch hazels, and wintersweet (*Chimonanthus praecox*).

11800 SW Military Lane, Portland, OR 97219, (503) 636-5613. Daily, 8–7 summer, 8–5 winter. From downtown Portland, take Hwy 14 (Macadam Ave) south to SW Military Rd; turn left and then immediately right onto SW Military Lane; Elk Rock is at the end of the lane.

Some labels; no restrooms; some wheelchair access; free.

The Grotto
PORTLAND

Asian and Middle Eastern gardens often seem charged with spiritual significance. Japan's Zen gravel and stone gardens, for example, illustrate the spatial experience of enlightenment, while the great gardens of Islam (the Persian term for garden, *paradeiza,* means paradise or heaven) typically feature formal stone watercourses representing the four rivers of life that flow between heaven and earth. In these gardens the landscape itself is used to express spiritual insights or experiences.

The West has also developed ways to express spiritual themes in gardens. Monastic gardens in the Middle Ages often were laid out in the shape of the cross, sometimes with a fountain at the center to symbolize the virgin birth of Christ, and many of the first botanical gardens in western Europe were meant to replicate the lost Garden of Eden. Today, however, few European or American gardens address spiritual or religious themes directly through, say, the use of religious statuary. Rather, they tend to address spiritual themes only on a subliminal level—that is, the harmony and tranquility of beautiful gardens are expected to inspire reflection and contemplation in visitors.

The Grotto, established in the 1920s by the Order of the Servants of Mary, combines aspects of these approaches on a 62-acre site featuring dramatic rock cliffs and panoramic views of Portland and the Cascade Mountains. Much of the site remains natural landscape, with Douglas firs, other evergreens, and bigleaf maples making a handsome backdrop to native ferns, groundcovers, and wildflowers. Woodland paths wander among religious statues at the base of the cliff; a 10-story elevator climbs the cliff to a sequence of garden areas, including a rose garden and beds of annuals, that are dotted with more statues and shrines.

A series of reflecting pools uses the landscape to express spiritual perceptions in the spirit, if not in the style, of Oriental gardens. A placard in the garden explains that the ponds and the stream that connects them represent the life-giving waters of baptism and spiritual regeneration. Don't overlook the sunken ponds fringed in daylilies and waterside perennials that border the parking lot.

8840 NE Skidmore St, Portland, OR 97220, (503) 254-7371. Mailing address: P.O. Box 20008, Portland, OR 97220. May–Sept, daily 9–6; Oct–Apr, Mon–Fri 10–4:30, Sat–Sun 9–5. From downtown Portland, take Burnside Bridge to Burnside Ave; turn left on Sandy Blvd NE, travel east to NE 85th St exit, and follow signs.

Brochure; guided tours by arrangement; gift shop; restrooms; wheelchair-accessible throughout; free (nominal fee for elevator to top of bluff).

Hoyt Arboretum
PORTLAND

 Portland's Hoyt Arboretum offers visitors an intriguing combination of native and exotic deciduous trees displayed against the somber greens of a notable collection of conifers. Located on a 175-acre site that covers a low ridge of the Tualatin mountain range, the arboretum seems spacious, by virtue of borrowing the scenery of two adjoining parks, and wild, because it features large communities of native plants left among the planted exotics.

SIGNIFICANT FEATURES

- ◆ the largest collection of conifers in the United States
- ◆ recent plantings organized by habitat and geography
- ◆ an extensive network of trails

HISTORY

Founded in 1928 and administered by Portland's Bureau of Parks and Recreation, Hoyt features ten miles of trails and excellent tree signage. Traditionally, the arboretum has arranged its trees taxonomically, or by plant family, with Fairview Boulevard, the main thoroughfare, bisecting the collections into gymnosperms (the conifers) and angiosperms (the flowering trees). In recent years, however, Hoyt has been moving from this type of arrangement to plantings based on geography or on various other themes. Collections of trees and other plants native to several distinct geographical areas are being added, including those typically found in a Chilean forest, a Tasmanian eucalyptus forest, an English beech forest, and a Yunnan Valley forest.

THE GARDEN PLAN

The visitors' center on Fairview Boulevard serves as a hub for footpaths radiating through the arboretum; each path bears the names of the tree collections through which it passes. The **Redwood-Spruce Trail** loops around Hoyt's extensive conifer collection, representing over 230 species, including fine stands of redwoods (*Sequoia sempervirens*) and incense cedars (*Calocedrus decurrens*), as well as rare examples of Brewer's weeping spruce (*Picea breweriana*), Himalayan spruce (*Picea smithiana*), and bristlecone pines (*Pinus aristata*). The **Oak Loop** takes visitors on a tour of the arboretum's deciduous trees, including collections of oaks, maples, and magnolias. Other trails wind through extensive natural areas, where signed exotics occasionally accent the mostly unsigned native plantings; on a recent visit, we felt like wild pigs gleefully seizing upon a truffle whenever such a sign came into view.

Hoyt Arboretum's collections based on geographical origin require painstaking research, since the staff must verify that all plants included in such groupings not only come from the same geographical region but also are naturally associated in the wild. Once the plant material has been targeted for inclusion, acquisition can also be a significant challenge. Hoyt has joined with Washington Park Arboretum in Seattle in an exchange of hard-to-find cuttings and seedlings in order to build up its new collections.

Collections arranged according to theme include a recent planting of summer-flowering shrubs and the **Winter Garden** located near the magnolia collection, northeast of the visitors' center. In the future, the arboretum plans to establish a collection of hardy bamboos along a creek and small ravine between the **Bristlecone Pine Trail** and **Himalayan Pine Trail,** northwest of the visitors' center.

BEST TIMES TO VIEW

Flowering cherries, pears, and crabapples dominate the arboretum in spring. The magnolia collection of 37 species blooms from March through late summer. Fall offers visitors vibrant seasonal foliage from late September to early November, with the show usually peaking during the last two weeks of October. To view a special autumn color display, walk the **Maple Trail** to a point several hundred feet north of its conjunction with the **Wildwood Trail** (just north of the parking area at the Wildwood trailhead). There a stand of Japanese and common persimmons (*Diospyros kaki* and *D. virginiana*) flames against a background of golden Lombardy poplars (*Populus nigra* 'Italica').

400 SW Fairview Blvd, Portland, OR 97221, (503) 823-3655. Daily 6–10 (visitors' center 9–3 most days). From I-5, take I-405 exit to Hwy 26W, then take Zoo-OMSI exit and follow signs.

Labels; brochures; guided tours; group tours by reservation; programs; picnic facilities; restrooms; some wheelchair access; free.

International Rose Test Garden
PORTLAND

Portland has had a long love affair with the rose. As early as the 1890s civic leaders had established an annual Festival of Roses, a horticultural society called The Mystic Order of the Rose was giving out free cuttings to homeowners, and public gardens and planting areas featuring roses were sprouting throughout the metropolitan area.

In 1914 three prominent eastern nurserymen, drawn to Portland's excellent growing conditions for roses, established a rose test garden in Washington Park. Within several years Portland's Bureau of Parks and Recreation took over its maintenance and development, and the garden now serves as a testing ground for the American Rose Society (especially miniatures) and the All-America Rose Selections (new hybrids), as well as for roses imported from England and other countries.

Today the 4½-acre garden supports over 400 labeled varieties of roses, planted on three broad terraces looking over Portland's skyline; stone fountains, grassy paths, and shallow flights of stone steps add backbone to the planting beds. The roses bloom from June through October. The adjoining Shakespearean Garden features trees, shrubs, perennials, and wildflowers referred to in the plays.

400 SW Kingston Blvd, Portland, OR 97201, (503) 248-4302. Daily 9–6. From I-5, take I-405 exit to Hwy 26W; take Zoo-OMSI exit to Washington Park and follow signs.

Restrooms; wheelchair-accessible throughout; free.

Jenkins Estate
ALOHA

The estate originally was the country property of Ralph and Belle Ainsworth Jenkins, a prominent Portland couple who acquired it around the turn of the century for use as a weekend retreat and horse ranch. In 1913 the Jenkinses moved to the estate year-round, built the main house, and began planting gardens in traditional English style. For the next 50 years professional gardeners developed and maintained perennial beds, wildflower meadows, rockeries, cutting beds, and ponds, most of them near the main house. Much of the rest of the estate's 68 acres remained natural woodland, although northwest of the main house a forest path led to a lilac walkway bordered by cutting beds.

The property endured a period of neglect between 1963, when Mrs. Jenkins died, and 1975, when the Tualatin Hills Park and Recreation District purchased the property. Today the district, assisted by area volunteers, is renovating those areas of the gardens for which plans from the Jenkins era exist. Other areas for which no plans are extant will be developed to take advantage of the site's topography and growing conditions; one new project is a rhododendron walk near the perennial garden.

The area of ponds, rockeries, and wood bridges northeast of the main house currently feels like the most "done" part of the renovation; it features the cohesive design and sympathetically arranged palette of plants that characterizes a true garden. Nearby, mixed shade borders of woodland shrubs and groundcovers look sweet and inviting in early summer, when astilbes, goat's-beard, foxgloves, and campanulas bloom together. West of the main house, at the end of an unpaved road, lies an herb and rose garden that was begun in 1986. The herb garden, whose design changes every year, features plants selected for their scent and texture; the roses are all species that were available to gardeners in 1913, the year the Jenkinses started their gardens.

Grabhorn Rd at SW 209th and Farmington Rd. Mailing address: P.O. Box 5868, Aloha, OR 97006, (503) 642-3855. May 31–Sept 30, Mon–Thurs 9–8, Fri 9–4; Oct 1–May 30, Mon–Fri 9–4. From Portland, travel west on Hwy 26 to 185th St exit; follow 185th to Farmington Rd and turn right; just before 209th St, turn left onto Grabhorn Rd; drive ¾ mile to garden entrance on right.

A braille wall in the herb garden identifies the plants; self-guiding brochure; guided tours by arrangement; classes and other events; restrooms, limited wheelchair access; free.

John Inskeep Environmental Learning Center
OREGON CITY

Gardeners used to be defined, quite simply, as people who loved plants and stuck them around their gardens in more or less pleasing arrangements: a straightforward understanding of how plants worked and some aesthetic sense earned you entry into the ranks of the blessed. Today gardening is a more complex business, with increasing numbers of gardeners considering themselves stewards of the land whose choices concerning plants, construction materials, and use or nonuse of chemicals create a significant ecological impact in their gardens. But acquiring information to make the right choices isn't always easy.

A visit to the John Inskeep Environmental Learning Center is a good way to start or expand your education as an environmentally sensitive gardener. This

8-acre learning center on the grounds of Clackamas Community College demonstrates a fascinating variety of ways to manage the garden environment through conservation of resources. Itself reclaimed from industrial wasteland, the center's campus is a patchwork of ponds and woods that serves as a wildlife sanctuary with exhibits of birds of prey and fish-rearing facilities. The campus and adjacent facilities also feature demonstration areas for composting yard debris, building solar-heated greenhouses, and constructing garden features with recycled plastics; a nursery selling wetland and wildlife-enhancing plants; a home orchard management station; and a sculpture garden in which the works of art are made from recycled metal, brass, copper, stainless steel, and concrete. Some nicely billowing, labeled perennial borders can be seen on the Clackamas Community College campus behind a hedge near the playing fields. A compost demonstration area, some beds of annuals, and an All-America Display Garden for veggies are located on the same site.

19600 S Molalla Ave, Oregon City, OR 97236, (503) 657-6958. Campus grounds are open daily during daylight hours; facilities hours vary, so phoning ahead is recommended. From I-205, take exit 10 and follow State Hwy 213 to Beavercreek Rd; turn left into Clackamas Community College. Extensive community education program; call (503) 657-6958 ext. 351 or 357 Tues–Sat 8–5 for a current schedule or to arrange site tours.
Campus restrooms; wheelchair-accessible throughout; free.

Leach Botanical Garden
PORTLAND

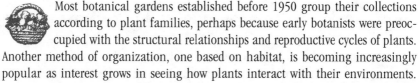 Most botanical gardens established before 1950 group their collections according to plant families, perhaps because early botanists were preoccupied with the structural relationships and reproductive cycles of plants. Another method of organization, one based on habitat, is becoming increasingly popular as interest grows in seeing how plants interact with their environments. This approach permits the display of plants in more diverse and natural arrangements than does traditional taxonomic grouping. Leach Botanical Garden, which groups many of its plant collections according to their growing requirements, features over 1500 plant species and cultivars in a variety of habitats spread over 9 acres of woodlands, rockeries, ravines, and wetlands in southeast Portland.

SIGNIFICANT FEATURES
+ bog, woodland, rock, and riparian habitats

- collections of Pacific Northwest natives, iris species, ferns, and azaleas native to the southeastern United States

HISTORY

When John and Lilla Leach married in 1913, she was a botanist trained at the University of Oregon and he was a public-spirited pharmacist with a decided knack for handling mules. Lilla was to find this latter skill invaluable over the next 20 years as she and John developed an extraordinary collection of Pacific Northwest native plants during extended mule-train trips through the back country of Oregon and Washington. During these trips Mrs. Leach discovered two new genera and eleven species, including such valued garden additions as the *Iris innominata* and dwarf shrub *Kalmiopsis leachiana*.

The Leaches acquired the site of the present garden (which they called Sleepy Hollow) in the 1930s, and there developed a series of habitats in which to grow their Northwest natives as well as their expanding collections of winter-blooming plants, groundcovers, camellias, viburnums, and witch hazels.

In 1972 the Leaches made a gift of their garden to the city of Portland; after Mrs. Leach's death in 1980, a nonprofit organization named the Leach Garden Friends joined with the city to manage the garden and its associated educational and conservation activities.

THE GARDEN PLAN

Leach Botanical Garden displays over 1500 varieties of plants (about 125 of them Pacific Northwest natives) planted along a 1½-mile path that winds through areas replicating the conditions of several different natural habitats. A dry native woodland habitat on the slope north of the entrance features a canopy of native firs, which provides filtered sunlight to a sub-story of native shrubs attractive to birds and a wide range of shade-loving native groundcovers. The woodland habitat is bordered to the north by a wildflower garden and to the south by a collection of native and exotic hardy ferns.

A rock garden on the north slope above the house contains plants that require sunny conditions and fast-draining soils, including alpines, wild native grasses, cacti, and succulents. On the south side of the house, which faces Johnson Creek, a shady rock garden displays ferns and other woodland perennials that require moist soils. Just below the shady rock garden is a bog garden with native Northwest swamp and wet-meadow plants. A riparian area bordering the creek features native trees and shrubs that can withstand repeated flooding, including willows, ashes, and black cottonwoods. Across Johnson Creek, a moist woodland area supports native vegetation that needs shade and humidity.

Other collections in the garden include plants naturally found in a xeric (dry) habitat, plants native to Curry County in southwest Oregon, and a taxonomic grouping of plants discovered by Lilla Leach.

BEST TIMES TO VIEW

The garden is interesting year-round; spring and early summer offer displays of blooming camellias, azaleas, and wildflowers.

6704 SE 122nd Ave, Portland, OR 97236, (503) 761-9503. Tues–Sat 10–4, Sun 12–6. From I-205, take Foster Rd exit (exit 17), travel east on Foster Rd to SE 122nd, turn south, drive about ⅛ mile, cross Johnson Creek, and look for parking lot on right.

Labels; excellent self-guiding brochures; visitors' center; programs, classes, activities; restrooms; limited wheelchair access; free.

Lewis and Clark College Campus
PORTLAND

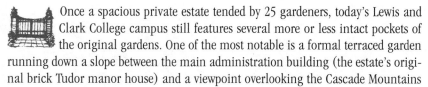 Once a spacious private estate tended by 25 gardeners, today's Lewis and Clark College campus still features several more or less intact pockets of the original gardens. One of the most notable is a formal terraced garden running down a slope between the main administration building (the estate's original brick Tudor manor house) and a viewpoint overlooking the Cascade Mountains and Mount Hood.

The terraces are composed of alternating stone walls, formal pools, and expanses of lawns whose interlocking patterns are punctuated by pergolas and brick and stone paths. A restricted palette of native firs, Atlas cedars, and Japanese maples ties these hardscapes to the surrounding landscape, making for a classically restrained design of a type seldom seen in the region's public gardens. (The terraced gardens annexed to Hatley Castle in Victoria, B.C., are the only other examples that come to mind.)

0615 SW Palatine Hill Rd, Portland, OR 97219, (503) 768-7000. Daily during daylight hours. From I-5, take Terwilliger exit (exit 297) to Palatine Hill Rd and follow signs.

Campus restrooms; limited wheelchair access; free.

Portland Japanese Garden
PORTLAND

Naturalistic planting schemes, a plant palette composed of evergreens selected for form and texture rather than for color, the careful unfolding of successive scenes along winding paths, and the subtle incorporation of distant views into the immediate landscape—these are the principles of design Westerners are accustomed to admiring in Japanese gardens.

Portland's garden offers superb examples of these principles, along with another feature that is seen more rarely in most North American Japanese-style gardens: impeccably designed hardscapes. Here the paths, walls, bridges, and fences—the structures that establish a Japanese garden's "bones"—are designed and executed with exceptional attention to detail. The resulting garden, a powerfully inspired combination of plants and constructed features, ranks among the region's, and the continent's, best.

SIGNIFICANT FEATURES
- five types of traditional Japanese gardens set in a hilly 5½-acre site
- remarkably beautiful hardscapes, many constructed with traditional materials and techniques

HISTORY
In 1962 a group of dedicated admirers of the Japanese approach to making gardens formed the Japanese Garden Society of Oregon. Within a year, they began planning the creation of a garden that would hug the ravines and promontories of a hilly site within Portland's Washington Park. The garden society commissioned the distinguished Japanese landscape architect Professor Takuma Tono to design a site plan that would feature several different types of traditional Japanese gardens while incorporating surrounding views of steep gullies, wooded slopes, and the Portland skyline.

Since its completion in 1967, Tono's garden has become widely recognized as a masterpiece of landscape design and garden ornamentation, and it is frequently cited as one of the most authentically styled Japanese gardens existing outside Japan.

Today the nonprofit society continues to develop and improve the garden; it also sponsors a year-round calendar of festivals and special events meant to deepen visitors' appreciation of the Japanese garden-making tradition.

THE GARDEN PLAN

Visitors approach the garden on a footpath that winds through Pacific Northwest woodlands to the entry gate, an imposing wood and tile construction built in the Daimyo style. (*Daimyos* were military lords in feudal Japan whose dwellings required fortified entries; the little box rooms on each side of the gate would have housed gatekeepers and soldiers.) Stone lions flank the gate: the male, holding down a stylized money pouch, represents power and wisdom, while the female, who rests her paw on a cub, represents guidance and protection. Symbolizing opposite yet complementary natural forces, these noble beasts act as fitting guardians to the perfectly realized universe that lies within the garden's walls.

Passing through the gate under the lions' protective scrutiny, visitors enter the garden proper on a path that curves gently to the left. The path leads to the **Flat Garden,** a rhythmic composition of stones, thyme, and sand that evokes an island-dotted sea. This sea is fringed by a rugged "shoreline" of pines, azaleas, and towering Douglas firs punctuated by rounded rocks that point into the sand like headlands jutting into the ocean.

Just behind the Flat Garden, the beautifully constructed wooden **Pavilion,** built in 1980, rides like a galleon in full sail above the swirling gravel seas. The Pavilion's east deck fronts a gravel terrace studded with massive slab stepping-stones; from this terrace visitors can enjoy panoramic views of Portland.

A path winding south from the terrace leads down into a hillside **Natural Garden,** the latest addition to the Portland Japanese Garden. Originally this area was a natural moss garden, but in the late 1960s the Japanese Garden Society decided to construct a series of ponds and waterfalls that would cascade down the hill through Northwest native trees, shrubs, and groundcovers. Designed by the garden's then landscape director, Portland-based landscape architect Hoichi Kurisu, the Natural Garden also has paths and walls made of stone and fences and gates made of bamboo and rough-cut cedar. These hardscapes flow into each other, and into the surrounding vegetation, as naturally and gracefully as streams curve down a hill.

Leaving the cascading paths, streams, and waterfalls of the Natural Garden behind, visitors approach the walled **Sand and Stone Garden,** whose elemental landscape—eight furrowed stones rising from a bed of speckled sand—seems, by contrast, as fixed and immutable as the surface of the moon. Traditionally, sand and stone gardens are attached to Buddhist temples, where their flat planes and bare surfaces echo the hard-edged lines of the buildings around them. Here trees surround the stone, stucco, and tile wall; when the light falls through their leaves to scatter shadows across the garden floor, the Sand and Stone Garden springs to rustling, flickering life.

After reclimbing the Natural Garden's crest, visitors walk down its other side to the **Strolling Pond Garden.** Designed in the same style as the sumptuous pleasure gardens of 16th- and 17th-century Japanese emperors, it features richly textured conifers, Japanese maples, weeping cherries, and sculpted evergreen shrubs fringing a complex of ponds and streams. These natural features are set off by gravel paths punctuated by granite stepping-stones, bamboo fences woven into delicate arches, and an elaborately carved wood bridge with cedar endposts capped by bronze lotus buds.

At the heart of the Strolling Pond Garden lies the **Tea Garden,** an exquisite miniature landscape built around an authentically constructed ceremonial teahouse. The complex relationships between specimen stones, stepping-stone paths, stone lanterns and water basins, and gravel terraces are handled with masterly ease in this area, making it a spot in which visitors love to linger.

BEST TIMES TO VIEW

Because Japanese gardens rely on evergreens for their basic structure, they can be visited with enjoyment at any time of year. The Portland Japanese Garden is open throughout the winter, when dripping conifers, glistening stepping-stones, and the sinuous branches of bare Japanese maples bring subtle beauty to the landscape. Spring and summer bring seasonal blooms: In mid-May (call for exact times year by year) a wisteria arbor makes a glorious display in full bloom, and in late June flowering iris border the stream in the Strolling Pond Garden.

611 Kingston SW, Portland. Mailing address: The Japanese Garden Society of Oregon, P.O. Box 3837, Portland, OR 97208, (503) 223-4070. Apr 1–Sept 30, daily 10–6; Oct 1–Mar 31, daily 10–4. Closed Thanksgiving, Christmas, and New Year's Day. From I-5, take I-405 exit to Hwy 26W, then take Zoo-

OMSI exit and follow signs.
Brochures; restrooms; limited wheelchair access; fee.

Sunken Rose Garden at Peninsula Park
PORTLAND

 This 2-acre rose garden, established in 1910, still features spacious formal planting beds edged in boxwood, a central fountain, brick walkways, and an elaborate old bandstand dating from that period. Visitors can view the sunken rose beds, planted in successive waves of white, cream, yellow, orangy-gold, and crimson blossoms, from stone balustrades that overlook the garden. The 10,000 plants established here include hybrid teas and floribundas; few are labeled. Roses are in bloom from June through October.

6400 Albina St, Portland; no phone. Daily during daylight hours. From I-5, take Portland Blvd exit (exit 304) and travel 3 blocks east on Portland Blvd to Albina St.
Restrooms; limited wheelchair access; free.

Tallina's Garden
CLACKAMAS

 At a certain point in the tractless desert of franchises and mini-malls lining Highway 224 between I-205 and Estacada, a gardener's mirage appears—a hill displaying hundreds of rose bushes surmounted by a latticed and domed gazebo garnished with stone nymphs and urns. Created by Tallina George on the grounds surrounding her doll's supply and lace shop, this 4-acre garden also includes water-lily pools, a knot garden, shady grape arbors, spacious perennial borders, and topiary giraffes. Built as a labor of love by the George family, the garden currently is being expanded to include a woodland area, with a pond and a stream, and a Victorian conservatory.

15790 SE Hwy 224, Clackamas, OR 97015, (503) 658-6148. Daily during daylight hours. From I-205, take Hwy 224 exit; travel east and watch for signs to Tallina's on north side of the road.
No restrooms; some wheelchair access; donation.

Washington Park Zoo Grounds
PORTLAND

Like the zoos in Tacoma and Seattle, Portland's Washington Park Zoo simulates the natural habitats of many of the animals it displays by using plants from Asia, Europe, the Mediterranean, and South America. A sculpture garden, a butterfly garden, and collections of bamboo, ornamental grasses, and species and hybrid lilies also make the grounds of interest to gardeners.

4001 SW Canyon Rd, Portland, OR 97221, (206) 226-1561. Daily, 9:30–7 summer, 9:30–4 winter. From I-5 traveling south, take I-405 exit to Hwy 26W, then take Zoo-OMSI exit and follow signs.
Restrooms; wheelchair-accessible throughout; fee.

WASHINGTON

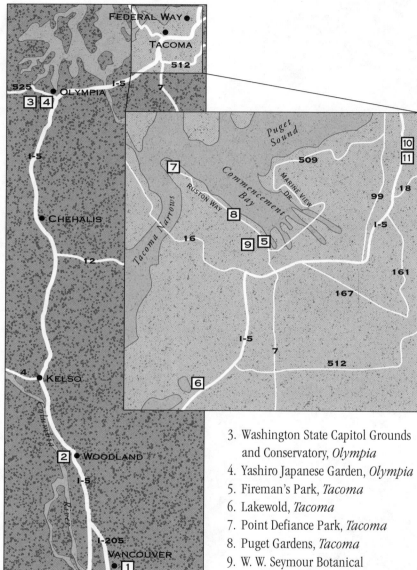

3. Washington State Capitol Grounds
   and Conservatory, *Olympia*
4. Yashiro Japanese Garden, *Olympia*
5. Fireman's Park, *Tacoma*
6. Lakewold, *Tacoma*
7. Point Defiance Park, *Tacoma*
8. Puget Gardens, *Tacoma*
9. W. W. Seymour Botanical
   Conservatory, *Tacoma*
10. Pacific Rim Bonsai Collection,
    Federal Way
11. Rhododendron Species Foundation
    Display Gardens, *Federal Way*

1. Pioneer Garden at Fort Vancouver
   National Historic Site, *Vancouver*
2. Hulda Klager Lilac Gardens,
   Woodland

Lakewold, *Tacoma*

SOUTHERN AND
CENTRAL WASHINGTON

Pioneer Garden
at Fort Vancouver National Historic Site
VANCOUVER

The Hudson's Bay Company established Fort Vancouver in 1824 as a supply post to fur traders active in the Oregon Territory. Before the fort was established, the main supply of food available to trappers and company employees was either imported from Europe or acquired by local hunting and fishing. The fort's first director, John McLoughlin (1784–1857), developed extensive on-site agricultural operations to supply fruits, vegetables, and grains to local residents and trappers. By 1846, the year McLoughlin retired, over 2500 acres surrounding the stockade were planted in wheat, oats, peas, and barley, and a nearby orchard contained 400 to 600 apple trees. During this same period, the fort's garden grew vegetables, flowers, fruits, and berries.

Today a portion of the Fort Vancouver garden has been reconstructed, chiefly by the efforts of volunteers, and it features plant varieties that research suggests grew in the original planting area. The garden is especially pretty in June, when old-fashioned perennials and flowering herbs are at their height of bloom.

E Evergreen Blvd, Vancouver, WA 98661, (206) 696-7655. Site, visitors' center, and restrooms: daily 9–5 in summer. Garden (located just outside the stockade): anytime. From I-5, take Mill Plain exit in downtown Vancouver, turn east, and follow signs to visitors' center.
Some labels; wheelchair-accessible; garden is free.

Hulda Klager Lilac Gardens
WOODLAND

Like Point Ellice House in Victoria, B.C., and the Hovander Homestead near Ferndale, Washington, this Victorian farmhouse and garden hearken back to a period early in the region's settlement. The pleasant old wood frame house, built before the turn of the century, has a front garden filled with mature maples, firs, cherries, plums, and magnolias interplanted with ornamental shrubs such as camellias, rhododendrons, hydrangeas, hollies, and boxwoods. Scattered drifts of cottage flowers—iris, columbines, foxgloves, daylilies, poppies, campanulas and yarrows—planted in free-form islands among the trees and shrubs, make this area look like an old-fashioned "grandma's garden"—one where common, well-loved flowering perennials scramble together in happy profusion.

But once visitors round the back of the house to view 530 lilac bushes lined up in neat rows, it becomes apparent that the Hulda Klager Lilac Gardens have an unusual past. This past highlights the important role dedicated amateurs sometimes have played in creating new varieties of ornamental plants for the region's gardens.

The story begins before the turn of the century, with the site's original owner, Hulda Klager. Mrs. Klager's family emigrated from Germany to the Midwest in the 1860s, and then moved west to settle in Woodland on the present site in 1877. After their marriage, Mrs. Klager and her husband farmed the land, brought up a family, and established a fine garden around the farmhouse. In 1903 Hulda read a biography of Luther Burbank and became inspired to hybridize fruit trees, roses, and shrubs in her own garden. Despite a lack of formal training and the demands of family and farm, she continued to hybridize plants, especially lilacs, for over 50 years, until her death in 1960. Eventually 64 of her hybrid lilacs were listed on the National Lilac Registry.

Using tiny brushes and a magnifying glass, Mrs. Klager would dab pollen on individual lilac blooms, and then hood each blossom with a bag to prevent cross-pollination by bees or the wind. She established starts from these plants in her test grounds, and evaluated them for hardiness, resistance to disease, and beauty of blossom. In a 1928 magazine interview, Mrs. Klager explained that if 1 in 400 starts was worth saving, she felt encouraged enough to continue her experiments.

Starting in 1920, Mrs. Klager held an annual open house during blossom time, during which the public could view her garden and purchase lilac starts; in this way, her new lilac varieties populated gardens all over the Pacific Northwest. After a disastrous flood in 1948 that destroyed every plant in the garden except several mature trees, clients from all over the region brought back starts of the lilacs they had purchased from Mrs. Klager, and she was able to recreate her collection.

The traditional open house continues today, sponsored now by the Hulda Klager Lilac Gardens Society, which saved the estate from threatened demolition in 1975 and currently maintains the gardens through volunteer efforts. During the annual Lilac Week (held during the first two weeks of May, depending upon bloom schedule) visitors may tour the Klager farmhouse, revel in the myriad scents of half a thousand lilac bushes, and purchase starts of the garden's various plants.

115 S Pekin. Mailing address: The Hulda Klager Lilac Gardens Society, P.O. Box 828, Woodland, WA 98674, (206) 225-8996. Daily, year-round, 9–5. From I-5, take Woodland exit (about 25 miles north of Portland); follow Goerig Rd to Davidson, turn right onto Davidson and then left onto S Pekin St; watch for garden sign on right.

Some labels; self-guiding brochure; no restrooms; limited wheelchair access; donation.

Washington State Capitol Grounds and Conservatory
OLYMPIA

The capitol's spacious grounds feature stands of flowering cherry trees, a glass conservatory displaying tropical and subtropical plants, a sunken garden filled with perennials and roses, and a collection of native and exotic trees. A brochure outlining each installation's location and history, as well as tour times for the conservatory and sunken garden, is available at the visitors' information center at the corner of Capitol Way and 14th Street near the entrance to the state capitol grounds.

The Washington State Capitol Museum, several blocks south of the capitol at 21st and Columbia, maintains a pioneer herb garden and a native plant garden on its grounds.

Capitol Way and 14th St. Information on hours and guided tours: State Capitol Information Center, Capitol Way and 14th St, Olympia WA 98504, (206) 586-8687. From I-5, follow signs to the state capitol.

Restrooms; wheelchair-accessible; grounds free.

Yashiro Japanese Garden
OLYMPIA

 This compact garden, which opened in 1990, was cooperatively planned over a seven-year period by the city of Olympia and its Japanese sister city, Yashiro. Sandwiched between the Olympia Chamber of Commerce Building and a gas station, it features a pleasant waterfall, fine wood entry gates, and a granite pagoda and several stone lanterns donated by the citizens of Yashiro. There are plans to add a traditional teahouse to the site in the future.

The garden centers on the waterfall, around which rise berms planted in rows of rhododendrons, azaleas, conifers, and other plants commonly found in Northwest parks and public gardens.

1000 Plum St, Olympia, WA 98501, (206) 753-8380 (Olympia Parks and Recreation Department). Daily, 10–10 (the garden is lighted at night). From I-5, take exit 105, travel toward the city center on Plum St (from the north, follow 105B once you are traveling on the 105 exit ramp); cross the first traffic lights on Plum St west of the freeway and look on the right hand side of the street for the Olympia Chamber of Commerce parking lot, which visitors can use while visiting the garden.

Brochures; guided tours by arrangement; no restrooms; wheelchair-accessible throughout; free.

Fireman's Park
TACOMA

A triangular park with old-growth firs and cedars existed at this down-town site overlooking Commencement Bay as early as 1891; during the next 40 years stone fountains and a bus terminal were added to the grounds. By the mid-1970s, however, the old-growth trees had been cut down and a freeway roared near the park's boundaries. At that time the Metropolitan Park District of Tacoma thoroughly upgraded the original site by bordering the side facing the street with a massive wall of rough boulders and by building pergolas and wood retaining walls along the side facing Commencement Bay. Stepping-stone paths and berms planted with shrubs divide the rock wall from the pergolas, making the long, narrow site seem both wide and spacious. Today visitors can enjoy sweeping views of the bay from a trellised promenade.

A St between S 8th and S 9th St in downtown Tacoma; no phone. Daily during daylight hours.
No restrooms; some wheelchair access; free.

Lakewold
TACOMA

England and the Continent are dotted with gardens that have been cher-ished, nurtured, and embellished over the course of centuries, with each new generation of gardeners seeking to complete and perfect the work of the gardeners who went before them. Because these new owners are working with already well-established gardens, their task (and a tricky one it can be) is to intro-duce changes into the landscape that express their individual tastes and sensibili-ties without violating the garden's spirit as it has developed through the work of the preceding owners. If the new owners are unable to tread this fine line, then their gardens can degenerate into a hodgepodge of styles and plants, and in consequence lose that sense of seamless unity of past and present which constitutes an old garden's chief charm.

Here in the Pacific Northwest few gardeners face this particular challenge since most of us work with gardens less than a generation old. But what about those among the region's gardeners who face the challenge of adding their personal touches to already well-established gardens? How do they add their own horticul-tural style to such a scene while preserving the integrity of the garden's original design and atmosphere? Lakewold, a 70-year-old formerly private estate now open to the public, demonstrates some instructive approaches to the problem.

SIGNIFICANT FEATURES

- ◆ a 10-acre lakeside estate with notable collections of rhododendrons, exotic trees, hardy ferns, and alpines
- ◆ a design created with the aid of the Olmsted Brothers and Thomas Church

HISTORY

The lakeside property now comprising Lakewold was bought in 1908 by Tacoma resident Emma Alexander as a setting for her summer cabin on Gravelly Lake. There was little alteration of the natural landscape during her period of residence; stands of Douglas firs and Garry oaks (*Quercus garryana*) were left to tower over other native trees, shrubs, and ground covers. In 1918 the property was transferred to Emma's son and daughter-in-law, H. F. and Ruth Alexander; they sold the site in 1925 to Everett and Grace Griggs, who lived there until the late 1930s.

During the tenure of the younger Alexanders and the Griggses, some rather formal gardens were established on the property. Designers from the Olmsted's landscape design firm created the handsome stone, wood, and ironwork fences and gates that surround the estate, as well as an elaborate brick pathway picked out in a herringbone pattern that still runs today between the house and the rose pergola. Photographs from this period show that native trees and understory were being cleared in order to establish rolling lawns, formal shrubberies, flower borders, and a rustic wood gazebo (which later became the teahouse). These features were designed much in the style of the contemporary East Coast estate gardens, which themselves were modeled along a more-or-less European country garden style.

In the late 1930s, the Griggses sold Lakewold to Corydon Wagner, Jr., and his wife, Eulalie Merrill Wagner, who were to garden there for the next fifty years. During their long tenure, the Wagners would modify the site they had acquired, with its conventionally attractive grounds, formal structural touches in fences, gates, and brick path, and groomed overstory of native trees, into a garden reflecting their unique interests.

As an initial reflection of their personal taste in plants, Corydon Wagner established a small arboretum of exotic trees on the grounds, while Mrs. Wagner added collections of rhododendrons, alpines, roses, and shade plants. Later the Wagners turned their attention to the problem of unifying the garden's overall design, and in the 1950s they commissioned Thomas Church to help them bind the property together into a cohesive and flowing site plan. During an association with the Wagners lasting over 25 years, Church designed a series of garden areas that gave the property organization and definition. These include the circular front driveway, formal parterres leading to the teahouse, several woodland glens, an herb garden, and the overlook in the rock garden.

THE GARDEN PLAN

Visitors enter Lakewold on Church's graveled front drive, which winds through Mrs. Wagner's exceptional collection of rhododendrons under-planted with native groundcovers. Selected primarily for their beauty of foliage texture and form, specimens of 170 species and 200 hybrid rhododen-drons have been sited here to create constantly unfolding woodland "rooms" and vistas.

Planted among the rhododendrons are trees chosen for their sophisti-cated color combinations. A stand of copper beeches (*Fagus sylvatica*) inter-planted with Japanese maples (*Acer japonica*) looks wonderful in spring, for instance, when their new leaves unfurl together in a cloudy mass of corals, russets, and bronzes. Farther on the delicate chartreuse foliage of a dawn redwood (*Metasequoia glyptostroboides*) complements the pale yellow blooms on a nearby Ukon cherry (*Prunus serrulata* 'Ukon') during the same season.

Mrs. Wagner also planted this area in trees that feature beautiful canopies of leaves—she was, we are told, a great believer in "looking up" when strolling through a garden, and consistently chose trees that reward vertical study.

The driveway ends in a courtyard before the Wagner's house, a Georgian-style mansion built with pale pink bricks. This part of the garden displays a dignified unity between the hardscapes—the house, drive, and courtyard—and the surrounding mature trees and shrubs. The floor of the driveway and courtyard is made of a fine gravel, which complements the classically proportioned house, clipped hedges, and moss-covered statues in the courtyard.

Moving around the house to the right, visitors encounter Mrs. Wagner's collection of roses, the Church-designed herb garden, informal perennial and wildflower beds, and rolling lawns which sweep down near the edge of Gravelly Lake. Here a rockery area, complete with waterfall, stream, and troughs, displays Mrs. Wagner's collection of native and exotic alpines.

From this point, a stroll through Corydon Wagner's adjoining arbore-tum, with its Persian ironwood (*Parrotia persica*), Chinese dove tree

(*Davidia involucrata*), Antarctic beech (*Northofagus antarctica*), Chilean fire tree (*Embothrium coccineum*), and various exotic firs, leads back up to the garden's most formal room. This area includes a complex of parterres bordering the Olmsted-designed brick path, a swimming pool, and a teahouse distinguished by tracery trellises, fine stone statues and benches, and a magnificent specimen of the climbing rose 'Kathleen,' which clambers over the dome.

In this area, the visitor well attuned to hardscape details may sense a certain lack of harmony in the setting. Is the flow of color and texture between the house's pink Georgian facade, the path's orangy-red Elizabethan brick, and the rustically romantic wood *treillage* of the teahouse entirely successful? Thomas Church attempted to unify these disparate elements by incorporating brick features into the nearby quatrefoil swimming pool, as well as by bringing the same quatrefoil design into his renovation of the teahouse floor. Church further attempted to unify these features by linking them with formal parterres and planting beds. These design solutions demonstrate how a gifted, innovative garden designer coped with the challenge of grafting different styles of hardscapes together in a garden setting.

BEST TIMES TO VIEW

In April and May rhododendrons, flowering cherries, tulips, azaleas, camellias, wisteria, and magnolias bloom. June brings peonies, roses, Himalayan blue poppies, and many kinds of flowering shrubs. During high and late summer, herbs, ferns, lush tree foliage, perennial borders and some annuals are on display. In autumn ornamental grasses, deciduous trees, asters, cyclamen, and fall crocus are at their best.

Friends of Lakewold, P.O. Box 98092, Tacoma, WA 98498, (206) 584-3360. Lakewold may be visited by reservation only, Apr 1–Sept 30; hours and days vary. Directions given at time reservation is made. (Lakewold is located on Gravelly Lake just south of Tacoma, off I-5.)

Some labels; brochure; guided or self-guiding tours, depending on day; gift shop; restrooms; limited wheelchair access; no children under 12; no pets; flat shoes required; fee.

Point Defiance Park

TACOMA

This 700-acre peninsula of woodlands pokes into Puget Sound like a stubby finger pointing at the Olympic Mountains on the distant horizon. The park features miles of trails that loop across virgin forest, sandy beachfront, and promontories with views of the Olympic Peninsula and islands in the sound. It includes display gardens and a zoo with naturalistic habitats that simulate bioclimates as diverse as the arctic tundra and a coral reef at low tide.

SIGNIFICANT FEATURES

- display areas of roses, dahlias, iris, and annuals, bordered by the Northwest forest primeval
- a Japanese garden
- a native plants garden

HISTORY

Military expeditions to Puget Sound in the 1840s immediately recognized the strategic significance of the peninsula now known as Point Defiance Park. "Give me fortifications and guns for the peninsula and I can defy the world," one early explorer said, thereby originating the peninsula's name. Congress designated the land as a military reservation in 1866. But the site remained unused for some 20 years, at which point the city of Tacoma petitioned the federal government for conveyance of title in order to establish a public park. Today 500 of Point Defiance Park's 700 acres still offer visitors an encounter—an increasingly rare encounter—with Pacific Northwest forestland virtually untouched by logging or other forms of human development.

THE GARDEN PLAN

The major plant display areas are located just inside the park's main entry. A pleasant pond and waterfall complex near the gate leads to a rose display area, first established in 1895, where labeled All-America Selections grow in beds surrounding a sturdy wood gazebo. Nearby are a compact iris display area created by the Tacoma Iris Society and several dahlia beds sponsored by the American Dahlia Society. Beyond the dahlia beds run a series of arched iron poles smothered in climbing roses; they create leafy, scented tunnels that open out into an annuals display garden with a stone wishing well located in its center.

Point Defiance Park also offers two gardens that pay homage to major influences on the region's developing garden "style": a Japanese garden and a native plants garden. The **Japanese Garden,** established in 1965, features pruned conifers and other evergreens sited around a stream and several ponds. The garden feels fresh and delicate in spring, when foliage is just uncurling; late-summer visitors may find it a little dusty and glum. Whatever time of year you choose to visit, note the remarkable giant redwoods (*Sequoiadendron giganteum*) near the central pond, and several unusually handsome stone lanterns scattered throughout the site. The wonderfully ornate pagoda that overlooks the Japanese Garden was built in 1916 as a streetcar-line terminus. Today, it can be rented for special events, and in late summer hundreds of cut dahlias from the nearby test garden are displayed here in a competition.

The 5-acre **Pacific Northwest Native Garden** was established by the Tacoma Garden Club in 1963 in an effort—farseeing for its time—to display Pacific Northwest native plants in a naturalistic yet cultivated setting. The original site featured steep hillsides converging on a ravine; six vegetation zones of the Pacific Northwest were planted, including habitats ranging from marshes and bogs to lowland coastal forests and eastern Cascade "steppes." Some of the most ornamental and garden-worthy plants native to the region are displayed here.

The animal and plant displays at Point Defiance Zoo illustrate how animals adapt to their environments. To this end, the display settings have been designed to look as natural as possible, with locally available look-alike plants sometimes simulating exotics too tender to grow in the Pacific Northwest. The zoo also boasts an extraordinarily beautiful view of Commencement Bay and its encircling forested shores.

BEST TIMES TO VIEW

The native garden blooms most profusely in spring; the display gardens are at their peak midsummer through autumn; the zoo and natural woodlands can be visited year-round.

5402 N Shirley Ave, Tacoma, WA 98407, (206) 591-5328. The park is open daily during daylight hours; call (206) 591-5333 for current zoo hours. From I-5 north of Tacoma, take the Hwy 16W (Bremerton) exit and follow the signs.

Picnic facilities; restrooms; wheelchair-accessible; free admission to park, fee for zoo.

Puget Gardens
TACOMA

 Originally a privately owned garden, this 3-acre site became a city park in 1986; it is currently administered by the Metropolitan Park District of Tacoma. Its main landscape features are a woodsy ravine, a stream with several ponds, and woodland slopes with boggy soils and shady exposures. John and Clara Skupen, the original owners, established candelabra primroses along the margins of the stream and ponds, and planted the rest of the grounds with rhododendrons, flowering cherries, azaleas, roses, and perennials. The best viewing time is late April, when spring flowers are at their peak.

3204 N Ruston Way, Tacoma, WA 98402, (206) 591-3690. Daily during daylight hours. From downtown Tacoma, travel north on N Ruston Way to Alder St, turn left, and look for the park on the left.
No restrooms; limited wheelchair access; free.

W. W. Seymour Botanical Conservatory
TACOMA

This deliciously Victorian conservatory is capped by a prismatic glass dome so airy that it seems to hover over the rest of the building like an iridescent bubble. Inside, almost 200 species of tropical plants, including bananas, guavas, figs, New Zealand tree ferns, palms, birds of paradise, and orchids reach toward the light in a junglelike tangle of lush foliage and brilliant blooms.

The conservatory was built in 1908 as a gift to the city of Tacoma by a regional magnate, William W. Seymour; the Metropolitan Park District of Tacoma recently has done a thorough renovation. Wright Park, in which the conservatory is sited, is a well-designed public landscape in its well-maintained peak of maturity; some of its exotic trees are over a hundred years old. The park is a great spot for a picnic on a hot summer's day.

316 G St, Tacoma, WA 98405, (206) 591-5330. Daily, 8:30–8 June 1–Labor Day; 8:30–4:30 rest of year; closed Thanksgiving and Christmas. From I-5 in downtown Tacoma, take exit 133 and follow signs for Route 705 N; take Stadium Way exit, turn left on 4th St, and follow G St to Wright Park.
Brochures; group tours by arrangement; seasonal displays; gardening workshops, plant and book sales; gift shop; restrooms; wheelchair-accessible; free.

Pacific Rim Bonsai Collection
FEDERAL WAY

 Closer cultural ties between the Pacific Rim nations are exposing more Pacific Northwesterners to the artistic treasures of the Far East. Few of these treasures are more intriguing than bonsai—the living jewels of Asia's horticultural tradition.

By the seventh century A.D. the Chinese had developed techniques for dwarfing trees and shrubs, calling them *penjing,* or pot plants, and during the next six centuries Japan imported and adapted these skills. Celebrated in poems and paintings ever since, bonsai are treasured in Asian cultures for representing nature in miniature. Just as haiku capture the essence of something much larger than their apparent subject, these miniature trees capture the essential qualities of their full-grown counterparts in nature.

Bonsai less than two feet high duplicate the twisting trunks and drooping branches of aged pines found on windswept mountains, the gnarled roots and moss-padded trunks of forest-dwelling maples, and the delicate flowers of a cherry tree in spring. Usually potted in shallow ceramic bowls and displayed in galleries like works of art, bonsai are living sculptures created in equal measure by nature and by human hands.

Pacific Northwesterners have found bonsai appealing from their first exposure to them about the turn of the century; currently the West Coast and Hawaii are centers of bonsai activity. The Pacific Rim Bonsai Collection is the largest and, at the same time, the most select group of bonsai now on display to the public in the western United States.

SIGNIFICANT FEATURES
- over 50 bonsai trees in a variety of styles
- an innovative facility specially designed for displaying and maintaining bonsai

HISTORY
When the Weyerhaeuser Company began planning a project to honor both the 1989 Washington State Centennial and the company's expanding cultural and trade relationships with Pacific Rim nations, the idea of establishing a bonsai collection of international significance caught and held the corporate imagination.

The collection, assembled by a task force of prominent American bonsai masters, represents a variety of countries, schools of style, and plant material, including examples of the Chinese and Japanese styles in both deciduous and evergreen specimens. The collection also includes tropical bougainvilleas and figs, specimens with interesting autumn berries, such as pyracantha, and many North American natives.

THE GARDEN PLAN

Once the scope of the collection was decided, Weyerhaeuser decided to locate the collection in an outdoor facility on an acre of forest land adjacent to the Rhododendron Species Foundation Display Gardens at the company's head-quarters in Federal Way. The facility was designed to blend naturally into its forest surroundings while housing specimen display areas, a greenhouse for overwintering tropical bonsai, and several offices.

The completed facility features a cluster of buildings and stucco walls that together form a central courtyard. The roof lines seem to float above the courtyard walls, acting as intermediary points between the tall forest canopy and the miniature bonsai.

The courtyard naturally funnels visitors into the bonsai display area immediately adjacent, where stucco walls separate and visually isolate the bonsai tables from one another. Heating coils are embedded in the tables so that bonsai can be protected in place during cold weather. Plaques on the walls contain information on the specimens. To visitors strolling the crushed-rock path between the displays, the bonsai resemble living jewels whose settings are enhanced by the cool, clear light filtering through the surrounding Douglas firs.

BEST TIMES TO VIEW

The collection was designed to be enjoyed year-round. The majority of specimens are evergreen junipers, pines, cedars, and firs, but flowering and fruiting bonsai add seasonal interest as well. In April, a 500-year-old Japanese mountain azalea (*Rhododendron serpylli-folium*) bears deep lavender flowers; in May a wisteria (*Wisteria floribunda*) blooms, and in late May or early June a 350-year-old Satsuki azalea (*Rhododendron* x *indicum*) bursts into pink flowers. A pomegranate (*Punica granatum*) blooms throughout the summer, followed by berried firethorn (*Pyracantha angustifolia*) in fall. Deciduous trees—maples, elms, and a crabapple—bear and drop their leaves seasonally. The bonsai look especially striking under snow, when their forms are highlighted.

P.O. Box 3798, Federal Way, WA 98063-3798, (206) 661-9377. Mar–Oct, Sat–Wed 11–4; Nov–Feb, Sun–Wed 11–4. From Seattle, take I-5 south to exit 142A to Hwy 18; travel east on Hwy 18 to Weyerhaeuser Way S exit, turn north on Weyerhaeuser Way, and follow signs.
Excellent labels; self-guiding brochure; programs; classes; gift shop; restrooms; wheelchair-accessible throughout; free.

Rhododendron Species Foundation Display Gardens
FEDERAL WAY

When turn-of-the-century Washington gardeners chose the Pacific rhododendron (*Rhododendron macrophyllum*) as the official state flower over its nearest rival (clover!), they were making the initial declaration in a love affair that still flourishes 90 years later. The mild, moist climate and acidic soils that characterize much of western Washington, western Oregon, and lower British Columbia create close-to-perfect growing conditions for both native and exotic rhododendrons—which may explain why they continue to be planted in our region's gardens and parks in a profusion outmatching that of any other flowering shrub.

The Rhododendron Species Foundation displays one of the world's largest collection of species rhododendrons in an attractive woodland setting just south of Seattle. (Species rhododendrons are the wild ancestors from which modern hybrids have been developed.) Strolling along the garden's paths in spring, when ruffled, tissue-thin blossoms ranging from wine-red to sunburst gold cascade down shrubs 20 feet tall, visitors get an unforgettable taste of rhododendron magic in full bloom.

SIGNIFICANT FEATURES
- over 500 varieties of species rhododendrons, most from Britain, the Himalayas, Japan, Korea, and China
- extensive companion plantings in a pond garden, an alpine garden, and flowering perennial borders

HISTORY

In 1964 the Rhododendron Species Foundation was established in a private garden in Eugene, Oregon, with the goal of creating a collection of species rhododendrons with superior forms and garden adaptability. In 1973 the Weyerhaeuser Corporation offered the foundation 24 acres on its head-quarters campus in Federal Way for a permanent display garden. When the foundation moved to its new home a year later, its mission expanded to pre-serving, growing, and distributing species rhododendrons that are threatened in their natural environments.

The foundation's expanded mission seems particularly timely. Today 850 known species of rhododendrons grow worldwide, in habitats as diverse as the timberline on Mount Everest and the steaming wetlands of Florida. But many rhododendron species are disappearing rapidly from their native environments, their existence threatened by encroaching human activity. To aid in their preservation, the foundation exchanges seeds and seedlings with horticulturists worldwide, grows endangered species for widespread distri-bution to botanical gardens, and advises countries seeking to preserve their wild rhododendron populations.

THE GARDEN PLAN

From the entry court, wood chip and gravel paths lead through the **Upper and Lower Study Gardens,** where species rhododendrons from each major group are displayed for comparative growth habit, leaf shape and tex-ture, and bloom. A woodland area canopied by native firs and Japanese maples leads visitors to the **Pond Garden,** where stands of bamboo, grasses, and waterside plants are planted on the rock-strewn margins of a pond. (An ambitious display of hardy ferns collected from around the world is currently being developed near the Pond Garden.) Continuing on the main path past the pond, visitors reach the gazebo, a wooden shelter perched on a slope overlooking the **Alpine Garden** and a sweeping lawn bordered by beds of perennials. The Alpine Garden features compact rhododendrons and other high-country plants that hug rocky outcrops and crawl across gravelly screes. Turning back toward the garden entrance, the path winds through displays of azaleas and a sale area where many plants found in the display gardens may be purchased for home cultivation.

BEST TIMES TO VIEW

Species rhododendrons bloom from January through July, but the greatest show of color occurs in March, April, and May. In summer the perennial borders and the Pond Garden are at their peak; this is also a good time to compare rhododendron leaf textures and shapes. The garden hosts a Fall Foliage Festival in October, when Japanese maples display their flamboyant autumn colors.

Rhododendron Species Foundation, P.O. Box 3798, Weyerhaeuser Way, Federal Way, WA 98063-3798, (206) 661-9377. Mar–Oct, Sat–Wed 11–4; Nov–Feb, Sun–Wed 11–4. From Seattle, take I-5 south to exit 142A to Hwy 18; travel east on Hwy 18 to Weyerhaeuser Way S exit, turn north on Weyerhaeuser Way, and follow signs.

Labels; brochures; guided tours Sun at 1 Mar–May; private tours by arrangement; gift shop; restrooms; some wheelchair access; fee.

A natural scene, *Olympic Peninsula*

OLYMPIC PENINSULA AND WHIDBEY ISLAND

Chetzemokah Park

PORT TOWNSEND

Fine old firs and shrubs, neatly laid out flower beds, and sweeping views of Puget Sound distinguish this 8-acre park in a quiet neighborhood above Port Townsend's downtown core. Established in 1904 by the Port Townsend ladies' Civic Improvement Club, the park at one time featured a zoo with bears and peacocks and a large ornamental pond with bronze turtles spitting water into the air. These glories have departed, but a crooked log bridge, a handsome gazebo, and log arbors covered in roses and vines still recall the park's Victorian heyday.

At the foot of Blaine St, on the bluff; no phone. Daily during daylight hours.

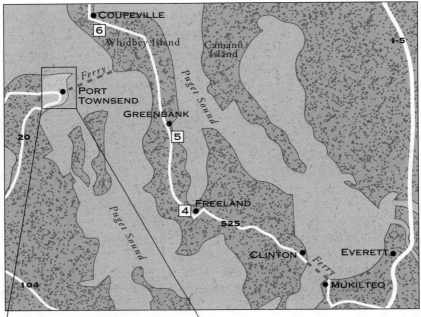

1. Chetzemokah Park, *Port Townsend*
2. Kah Tai Lagoon Nature Park, *Port Townsend*
3. Rothschild House, *Port Townsend*
4. Froggwell Garden, *Freeland*
5. Meerkerk Rhododendron Gardens, *Greenbank*
6. Rhododendron Park, *Coupeville*

From ferry terminal, turn right on Water St then left on Monroe St; continue up hill to Blaine St and turn right to park entrance.

Picnic tables; restrooms; some wheelchair access; free.

Kah Tai Lagoon Nature Park
PORT TOWNSEND

This 85-acre patchwork of wetlands, grasslands, and woodlands features interpretive displays and 2½ miles of trails.

12th St near Sims Way; no phone. Daily during daylight hours. From ferry terminal, turn left on Water St, which becomes Sims Way; continue on Sims Way until it crosses 12th St.

Picnic tables; restrooms; some wheelchair access; free.

Rothschild House
PORT TOWNSEND

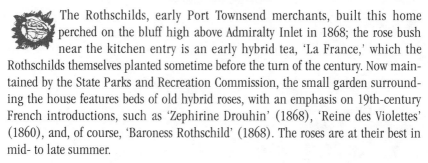

The Rothschilds, early Port Townsend merchants, built this home perched on the bluff high above Admiralty Inlet in 1868; the rose bush near the kitchen entry is an early hybrid tea, 'La France,' which the Rothschilds themselves planted sometime before the turn of the century. Now maintained by the State Parks and Recreation Commission, the small garden surrounding the house features beds of old hybrid roses, with an emphasis on 19th-century French introductions, such as 'Zephirine Drouhin' (1868), 'Reine des Violettes' (1860), and, of course, 'Baroness Rothschild' (1868). The roses are at their best in mid- to late summer.

Corner of Franklin and Taylor; no phone. Daily during daylight hours. From ferry terminal, turn right on Water St and then left on Quincy St; go up the hill to Franklin, and turn left to Taylor.

Some labels; no restrooms; some wheelchair access; garden is free; donation to tour the house.

Froggwell Garden
FREELAND

Spacious free-form beds filled with pastel blooms and boldly textured foliage form the heart of this 1-acre garden set in Northwest woodland. Owner Holly Turner has planted other areas with unusual rhododendrons, gold- and burgundy-leaved shrubs, ornamental natives, a fragrant herb garden, and an extensive winter-blooming border. A tour of this otherwise private garden is included in the 4-hour seminars Turner conducts on designing and maintaining perennial borders, mixed borders, and winter gardens.

5508 Double Bluff Rd, Freeland, WA 98249, (206) 221-7308.
Call or write for brochure describing the classes and fee information.

Meerkerk Rhododendron Gardens
GREENBANK

These gardens were started in 1963 by Max and Ann Meerkerk, world travelers who, on their retirement to Whidbey Island, had become fascinated by the native Pacific rhododendrons (*Rhododendron macrophyllum*) flowering freely in many of the island's woods. Their interest quickly expanded to other species of rhododendrons, and soon the Meerkerks determined to develop their homesite (which eventually came to cover 53 acres) as a preserve for rhododendrons and companion plants. As a former ambassador representing the German government, Max Meerkerk had extensive contacts in Europe and Asia, and through them he collected a core group of 50 rare rhododendrons, both species and registered hybrids, from all over the world. This collection, now named the Heritage Gardens, covers 5 acres of the present grounds. The Meerkerks also hybridized rhododendrons, and some of Ann's hybrids still flourish in the garden today.

The Meerkerks wanted the garden preserved after their deaths, so they arranged for the Seattle Rhododendron Society to take over its development; it opened as a public garden in 1979. Today display and hybrid test areas are being established near the main entrance. In the future, the society plans to enlarge the hybrid test gardens, establish a comprehensive collection of Asian rhododendrons, and plant a fern test garden. Much of the site will remain natural woodlands, crisscrossed by 4½ miles of trails.

P.O. Box 154, Greenbank, WA 98253, (206) 678-8740 or (206) 321-6682. April and May, Wed–Sun, 9–4. From Seattle, take Mukilteo ferry to Clinton; drive north on Hwy 525 for approximately 15½ miles, turn left on Resort Rd, travel ¼ mile, and turn left at sign.

Labels; self-guiding brochures; guided tours by arrangement; toilet; limited wheelchair access; fee.

Rhododendron Park
COUPEVILLE

Visitors can see significant stands of our native Pacific rhododendron in full bloom (usually in mid- to late May) in Rhododendron Park just south of Coupeville. The park is part of a 160-acre complex of camping and recreation facilities located in some unspoiled Northwest forest land. It's a great spot for a picnic, even with the eerie background whistle of aircraft taking off from a nearby military base.

From Coupeville, drive south on Hwy 20 approximately ½ mile, and turn right into a gravel driveway marked only by a triangular campground sign. Daily, dawn to dusk.

Restrooms; limited wheelchair access; free.

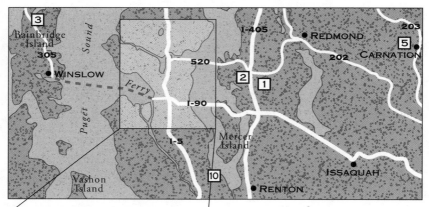

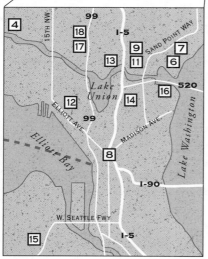

6. Center for Urban Horticulture, *Seattle*
7. Children's Hospital and Medical Center Perennial Borders, *Seattle*
8. Downtown Gardens, *Seattle*
9. Erna Gunther Ethnobotanical Garden, *Seattle*
10. Kubota Gardens, *Seattle*
11. Medicinal Herb Garden, *Seattle*
12. Parsons Gardens, *Seattle*
13. Tilth and Good Shepherd Demonstration Gardens, *Seattle*
14. Volunteer Park Conservatory, *Seattle*
15. Walker Rock Garden, *Seattle*
16. Washington Park Arboretum and Japanese Garden, *Seattle*
17. Woodland Park Rose Garden, *Seattle*
18. Woodland Park Zoological Gardens, *Seattle*

1. Bellevue Botanical Garden, *Bellevue*
2. Bellevue Downtown Park, *Bellevue*
3. Bloedel Reserve, *Bainbridge Island*
4. Carl S. English, Jr., Botanical Gardens, *Seattle*
5. Carnation Research Farm Gardens, *Carnation*

Bloedel Reserve, *Bainbridge Island*

SEATTLE AND ENVIRONS

Bellevue Botanical Garden

BELLEVUE

The region's newest botanical garden is a 36-acre complex of display and demonstration gardens and natural woodlands in Bellevue's Wilburton Hill Park. The garden presently features a half-mile loop trail that takes visitors through a 7-acre collection of mature species and hybrid rhododendrons, a groundcover garden complete with stream and ponds, a wetlands area, and a massive perennial border featuring outstanding color and foliage combinations. Future projects include a "water-wise" garden, a bog garden, an alpine scree, and an Asian garden that will showcase plants native to Asia established in a naturalistic setting of woodlands and ponds.

The botanical garden had its beginnings in 1980, when Calhoun and Harriet

Shorts donated their private 7-acre rhododendron garden atop Wilburton Hill for use as a public space. The City of Bellevue Department of Parks and Recreation combined the Shortses' original contribution with some surrounding parkland; aided by the volunteer Bellevue Botanical Garden Society, it is now developing the demonstration gardens and a public education program that will include lectures, workshops, and plant sales.

12001 Main St. Mailing address: Bellevue Botanical Garden Society, P.O. Box 7081, Bellevue, WA 98008, (206) 451-3755. Daily 10–6. From I-405, take NE 8th St exit, travel east to 116th Ave NE, turn right (south) and continue to 1st St, turn left (east) and continue on 1st as it becomes Main St.

Labels; group tours by arrangement; visitors' center; programs; classes; giftshop; restrooms; wheelchair access; free admission at press time, but fees may be imposed at a later time.

Bellevue Downtown Park
BELLEVUE

This 20-acre park occupies a square block just south of the downtown Bellevue shopping core. In contrast to most of the region's more naturalistic parks and gardens, the park features a deliberately formal design meant to complement its urban setting. Its "circle within a square" layout includes a grass meadow encircled by a stone-lined canal and a walkway punctuated by London plane trees. The canal leads down, via a series of shallow water steps, to a formal reflecting pond in the southwest corner of the park. The northeast quadrant is the most built-up part of the park; it features a rather opulent stone terrace from which visitors can view the entire park, and a small side garden with formal beds of perennials and herbs. Future developments will include an amphitheater, a children's play area, and a grove of flowering cherries leading to a memorial honoring Japanese-American citizens who were World War II camp internees.

Intersection of Bellevue Way and NE 4th St, just south of Bellevue Square; no phone. Daily during daylight hours. From I-5 in Seattle, travel across Lake Washington on Hwy 520 and take Bellevue Way exit to downtown Bellevue. Parking is at southwest corner of park near NE 1st and 100th Ave NE.

Restrooms; wheelchair-accessible; free.

Bloedel Reserve
BAINBRIDGE ISLAND

 In 1730 Lord Bathurst wrote to his old friend Alexander Pope, begging the poet to come and visit him at his vast estate in Gloucestershire. Both men were devoted gardeners, and Bathurst sweetened his invitation with a playful bribe: "I'll cutt you off some little corner of my Park (500 or 1000 acres) which you shall do what you will with, & I'll immediately assign over to you three or four millions of plants out of my Nursery to amuse yourself with."

It's an offer that would tempt any serious gardener: unbounded space and unlimited means with which to create his or her own private Eden. Prentice and Virginia Bloedel were presented with a similar opportunity when they acquired a 150-acre tract of forest land on Bainbridge Island near Seattle in 1951. During the next 30 years the Bloedels, with the assistance of such eminent landscape architects as Thomas Church and, later, Richard Haag, created an intriguing "garden in the forest," an artful woodland tapestry influenced by the native landscape and by Japanese and European gardening traditions.

Walking along the reserve's two miles of trails, visitors encounter a complex yet flowing succession of broad meadows, narrow ravines, deep woods, and mysterious glens—all of them serving as natural backdrops to more formal garden areas that include a Japanese garden and a grandly geometric reflecting pool.

SIGNIFICANT FEATURES

- ◆ a series of garden rooms established in the heart of a Pacific Northwest forest
- ◆ the ornamental use of Pacific Northwest native plants in combination with complementary exotics
- ◆ President's Award of Excellence, American Society of Landscape Architects, for outstanding garden design

HISTORY

When the Bloedels bought the large tract of land and the severely elegant French chateau that stood on it, the landscape was a second-growth tangle of mixed conifer and hardwood stands, wetlands, streams, and brush. According to Mr. Bloedel's published statements, " [at first] we were scarcely aware of the land itself." During their long rambles over the property in all seasons of the year, however, "it wasn't long before we found the land marvellously varied in contour and physiography. . . . A world of incomparable diversity, exciting in its vitality." When the time came to establish gardens on the property, Bloedel insisted that a similar spirit of appreciation for the beauty and integrity of the natural landscape inform the proposed plans.

Determined to create a garden that embodied the qualities of naturalness, subtlety, and tranquility, the Bloedels rejected many garden projects over the following years as too manipulative of the landscape. Instead, they sought designs that would free "what was inherently there in the landscape . . . [in order to make] a garden that never appears self-conscious or obtrusive, but seems to belong to the place." This spirit of intelligent and sensitive cooperation with nature constitutes one of the reserve's greatest attractions.

Today the Bloedel Reserve is open to the public; the Arbor Fund, a nonprofit organization endowed by the Bloedel family, operates it and administers the reserve's further development.

THE GARDEN PLAN

A little more than half the site has been left as natural landscape, with paths winding through forest, meadows, marshes, and ponds. Although the heart of the reserve remains wild, it has a series of planned garden rooms whose designs emphasize natural and unforced transitions from one room to another.

In 1956 the Bloedels commissioned Seattle landscape designer Fujitaro Kubota to create the **Japanese Garden.** Located in a broad ravine with a large central pond, the garden features a classic blend of clipped pines, massive boulders, and winding paths. A guest house whose design was inspired by both Japanese temple architecture and Native American longhouse construction overlooks the garden. A slope leading from the guest house down to the pond is one of the Japanese Garden's most attractive areas, with mossy banks bordering small streams and a dry waterfall of cascading pebbles.

The nearby **Moss Garden,** begun in 1982 by Richard Haag, is a unique landscape of Scotch and native mosses that have been allowed to crawl up the trunks of alders and bigleaf maples, engulf the remains of rotting tree stumps, and swirl around the sword ferns (*Polystichum munitum*) and small boulders strewn across the garden floor. Skunk cabbages and thick plantings of devil's walking stick (*Aralia spinosa*) add a sinister touch to this dramatic garden room, which seems flooded with a somber light and the spicy scent of decay.

The path winding through the Moss Garden leads to the **Reflection Pool,** a nobly proportioned rectangle of dark waters hedged by clipped yews that was designed with the assistance of Thomas Church, Richard Haag, and

Prentice Bloedel himself. Formal, understated, reflecting the tips of the surrounding trees with delicate clarity, the pool feels like the center, the still
heart, of the garden complex.

During the process of establishing these garden areas and the links
between them, several different plans were adopted and then partially dis-
carded. As a result there is no generally agreed-upon route through them
that all the garden's designers, past and present, consider satisfactory.

Visitors may choose their own routes according to taste. To travel from
the wildest parts of the garden into its formal center, they might start near
the bird marsh (a large undeveloped area of meadows and ponds south of the
other gardens), loop through the Moss Garden to the Reflection Pool, and
finish their tour in the Japanese Garden. An alternative route, starting at the
Japanese Garden, slows visitors down and makes them notice landscape
details. Then, once a calm and receptive frame of mind is established, a
stroll in the Moss Garden becomes especially thrilling on some deep and
atavistic level. A long ruminating pause at the Reflection Pool serves as
preparation for a finishing loop around the bird marsh.

Whichever route they follow, visitors should include a visit to the
chateau, now a visitors' center, for sweeping views of bluffs and the broad
waters of Hood Canal. On the way back from the visitors' center to the entry
gate, a final detour to the **Glen** reveals primroses, rhododendrons, bulbs,
and wildflowers blooming according to season.

There is great charm at work at Bloedel Reserve, partly because of the
appreciative restraint with which humans have laid their imprint on the
natural landscape, and partly because the reserve, although conceived on a
large scale, nevertheless preserves a personal and intimate mood. Even after
repeated visits, it's the kind of garden that takes up permanent residence in a
corner of one's mind.

BEST TIMES TO VIEW

Bloedel Reserve offers wonderful attractions year-round, from winter's
conifers, bark, and berries to early spring's trillium and cyclamen, through
summer's wildflowers, to leaf change in autumn. Species and hybrid azaleas
and rhododendrons, flowering crabapples, cherries, dogwoods, and magnolias flower in spring. During April and May, apricot- and wine-colored
primroses and Virginia bluebells cover the floor of the Glen, while stewartias
blossom with camellialike flowers in late May. Changing katsura trees and
Japanese maples make the Japanese Garden well worth a visit in fall.

7571 NE Dolphin Drive, Bainbridge Island, WA 98110-1097, (206) 842-7631. Year-round, by reservation only, Wed–Sun, 10–4, except holidays. Directions given at time of reservation.

Maps; restrooms; some wheelchair access; fee.

Carl S. English, Jr., Botanical Gardens
SEATTLE

When botanist Carl S. English, Jr. first joined the staff at the Hiram M. Chittenden Locks in 1931, the grounds featured a standard—and unexciting—combination of lawns and common ornamental trees. Over the next 43 years, English transformed the 7-acre grounds into a treasure house of over 500 varieties of exotic trees and shrubs, many of them grown from seeds that he obtained from such diverse corners of the world as Thailand, New Zealand, China, South America, and Japan. English also took a great interest in plants native to western North America, and he planted native conifers on the grounds from seeds collected on personal expeditions throughout the western United States. Today the principal plant collections include heathers, maples, oaks, and magnolias. Rhododendrons, pines, and stewartias also grace the grounds, and there are rose and perennial beds behind the main administration building.

Hiram M. Chittenden Locks (also called Ballard Locks), 3015 NW 54th St, Seattle, WA 98107, (206) 783-7059. Daily, year-round, during daylight hours. From 1-5, take NE 45th St exit (exit 169) and travel west toward Ballard, following signs for Chittenden Locks.

Labels; self-guiding brochures; guided tours by arrangement; snacks; restrooms; some wheelchair access; free.

Carnation Research Farm Gardens
CARNATION

In 1910 Elbridge Amos Stuart, a Seattle entrepreneur, bought several hundred acres of rich Snoqualmie Valley bottomland and over the next several decades built up a large research and breeding facility for prime milk-producing cows. By 1914 Stuart also had acquired a hillside above the original valley-floor property; on this slope he constructed a home for his family and a fine 3-acre garden consisting of formal rose and annual beds divided by stepping-stone paths, clipped evergreen hedges, and rustic wood pergolas and trellises.

The gardens, now open to the public, make for a very pleasant country stroll, especially in July and August, when the roses and the beds of annuals are at their peak of bloom. Visitors may also want to visit the farm's buggy and carriage museum, maternity and nursery barns, and Labrador show-dog kennels.

Carnation Farm Rd, Carnation, WA 98104, (206) 788-1511. Apr–Oct, Mon–Sat, 10–3. From Seattle, take I-90 east, Hwy 202 to Fall City, and then Hwy 203 north; turn west on Carnation Farm Rd and follow signs.
   Self-guiding brochure; restrooms; limited wheelchair access; free.

Center for Urban Horticulture
SEATTLE

McVay Courtyard is an innovatively designed courtyard that stands amid the complex of offices and meeting rooms at the Center for Urban Horticulture. It features granite boulders and naturalistic plantings, with a sunken gravel and stepping-stone path swirling through its bermed center. Because the area is small, crowding it with a random hodgepodge of plants would have been easy. Instead, the plant selection was deliberately restricted to one type of tree, the Japanese maple (*Acer japonicum* 'Aconitifolium'); two evergreen shrubs with contrasting textures and growth habits, *Osmanthus delavayi* and *Arctostaphylos canescens;* and a variety of grasses and bamboos. The resulting planting scheme, graceful and unforced, rewards detailed study. For a small site completely enclosed by buildings, the garden feels flowing, spacious, and filled with light—subtle effects echoing Japanese, and even Chinese, traditions for designing courtyard gardens.

The center also features an attractive entryway garden, planted in unusual groundcovers and small ornamental trees, and the Goodfellow Grove, an area of native trees, shrubs, and marsh plants that fringes a handsome stone-lined water channel.

3501 NE 41st St, Seattle, WA 98109, (206) 543-8616. The Center for Urban Horticulture is open 8–5 weekdays year-round. (Usually the courtyard is closed after center hours.) From I-5, take NE 45th St exit (exit 169), travel east to Union Bay Circle, and turn right onto NE 41st St.
   Some labels; brochures; programs; classes; restrooms; some wheelchair access; free.

Children's Hospital and Medical Center Perennial Borders

SEATTLE

 These compact but delightful borders fringe a series of steps and landings on the slope that separates the covered parking lots from the hospital's main entrance. The sophisticated mix of common and unusual herbaceous perennials, grasses, and groundcovers is framed by a variety of deciduous and evergreen trees and shrubs, providing gardeners a cornucopia of delicious ideas to try at home. The rest of the hospital grounds features naturalistic planting schemes, many of them emphasizing native and drought-tolerant plants.

4800 Sand Point Way NE, Seattle, WA 98105, (206) 527-3889. Daily during daylight hours. From I-5, take NE 45th St exit (exit 169) and travel east; at Union Bay Circle, NE 45th St becomes Sand Point Way NE; look for signs to hospital on the right.
Hospital restrooms; limited wheelchair access; free.

Downtown Gardens

SEATTLE

The words "urban public garden" may seem a contradiction in terms, since such gardens often must accommodate constricted sites, limited views, harsh growing conditions, and less-than-meticulous maintenance. Designed by landscape architects who also must deal with such practical problems as limited budgets, public safety, damage control, and traffic flow, urban gardens seldom feature those intimate settings and choice plant palettes we think of as pre-eminent characteristics of the classic garden.

Yet what a well-designed urban public garden may lack in intimacy and interesting plantings is often compensated for by an exciting design that makes the best of a difficult site. Two leafy oases in downtown Seattle merit special attention because their ingenious designs successfully cope with the surrounding urban conditions.

Freeway Park is a dramatic concrete construct featuring cliffs, trees, and cascades that caps Interstate 5 just south of the Washington State Trade and Convention Center in downtown Seattle. The freeway, built through the downtown corridor in the mid-1950s, became a roaring urban river of traffic noise and pollution that cut off the city's core from a neighborhood of apartment buildings and medical complexes to the east. When landscape architect Angela Danadjieva was commissioned to design the park, she faced the interrelated problems of lidding the noisy freeway and of reconnecting downtown to the adjacent neighborhood. The site she had to work with was, quite literally, the space above the freeway—a 5-acre area with a vertical drop of 90 feet between its highest and lowest levels and an environment that promised extremely harsh growing conditions.

Danadjieva's solution was to design the park as a series of concrete canyons, cliffs, and watercourses connected by small sunny plazas, intimate corridors, and steep flights of stairs. A 30-foot waterfall and a series of white-water cascades drown out the noise of the freeway, while huge concrete "pots" installed at floor level hold a special lightweight soil mix that supports mature evergreens, oaks, and flowering shrubs. Blankets of ivy, echoing the water cascades nearby, soften many of the concrete walls, which have been textured to resemble rough wood. Trees and shrubs selected for their toughness have flourished in this environment, and some trees actually were removed in the early 1990s to prevent the site from appearing overgrown. After Freeway Park opened to great acclaim in 1976, Danadjieva urged the construction of more plazas, overhangs, and terraces to extend the park over most of Interstate 5 through downtown, envisioning the whole complex as "a green necklace floating over the freeway." Almost 20 years later, it still seems a vision worth carrying out.

At 6th Ave and Seneca St over I-5 in downtown Seattle; no phone. Daily during daylight hours. From I-5 northbound, take Seneca St exit; from I-5 southbound, take Olive Way exit.

No restrooms; some wheelchair access; free.

The Waterfall Garden, near historic Pioneer Square, is a small site (60 feet by 108 feet) dominated by a thundering 22-foot waterfall dropping from a massive wall of rubble. The waterfall's drama focuses the visitor's attention on garden fundamentals—stone and water, motion and light—and away from the nearby urban landscape. Designer Masao Kinoshita ran a shallow watercourse around the perimeter of the garden which both encloses it from the adjacent streets and acts as a formal counterpoint to the wild waterfall. Native shrubs rim the watercourse.

Corner of 2nd Ave S and S Main St; no telephone. Daily, during daylight hours. From I-5, take the James St exit and travel west to 2nd Ave; turn south on 2nd Ave to Main St.

Snack bar; no restrooms; wheelchair-accessible; free.

Erna Gunther Ethnobotanical Garden
SEATTLE

 Visitors to the University of Washington campus who are native plant enthusiasts may want to stop by the main entrance to the Thomas Burke Memorial Washington State Museum to view a small but well-labeled collection of Pacific Northwest plants that were used by the region's indigenous peoples for food, medicine, and tools. A self-guiding brochure to the collection is available in the museum lobby.

Corner of 17th Ave NE and NE 45th St. Information: Thomas Burke Memorial Washington State Museum, University of Washington DB-10, Seattle, WA 98195, (206) 543-5590. Collection, daily during daylight hours; museum, daily 10–5 (10–8 Thurs). From I-5, take NE 45th St exit (exit 169), and travel east to 17th Ave NE.

Labels; museum restrooms; wheelchair-accessible; collection free.

Kubota Gardens
SEATTLE

 Kubota Gardens represents a skillful adaptation of selected Japanese garden design principles to the landscape and plant palette of the Pacific Northwest. The 20-acre site is a broad ravine, about 5 acres of which are formal garden areas complete with ponds, waterfalls, bridges, and specimen plantings. Another 5 acres, with stands of firs, dogwoods, pines, and rhododendrons, serves as a transitional area between the formal areas and the remainder of the site, which is native woodlands and meadows.

Because it is one of Seattle's lesser-known and less-visited public gardens, Kubota retains a secluded and tranquil spirit; it's the spot to visit when one feels the need to ponder and reflect. Although the Pacific Northwest has many private gardens that combine traditional Japanese garden styles with a mix of Northwest natives and commonly planted exotics, Kubota Gardens ranks as one of our finer public examples.

SIGNIFICANT FEATURES

- ◆ a design that skillfully integrates formal and informal garden areas
- ◆ authentic Japanese prayer stones and stone lanterns

HISTORY

Fujitaro Kubota, a Seattle-based garden designer and nurseryman, developed the original 5-acre site in 1929 to serve both as a family garden and as a display area for his landscaping business. During the 1930s, Kubota Gardens featured formal lawns, ponds, and perennial borders, as well as stands of pines grown from seed collected in Japan.

Over the next 50 years Mr. Kubota acquired 15 acres of additional land. The original acreage continued as the core of the garden, with most of the added land either remaining wild or serving as bedding areas for the family nursery.

During World War II the Kubota family were interned at a camp in Idaho, and as a consequence the gardens entered a period of neglect. After the war ended, Mr. Kubota and his sons decided to renovate the core garden by building a series of rock outcroppings and water features—work that was completed by the early 1960s. After Fujitaro Kubota's death in 1973, his family found the garden's upkeep increasingly difficult. Its historical significance, however, was recognized by the city of Seattle in 1981, when the Seattle Landmarks Preservation Board designated the core garden an historical landmark.

The Kubotas had always allowed the public to visit their gardens informally, so when the property eventually was placed on the market, community sentiment favored its purchase by the Seattle Parks and Recreation Department rather than by private parties. The Department acquired the gardens in 1987 and has embarked on a vigorous renovation; it is currently considering their further development.

THE GARDEN PLAN

The original 5-acre core parcel, located along Renton Avenue South, remains the heart of Kubota Gardens today. In this area, graveled paths alternating with half-buried stepping-stones wander through quite formal settings of ponds and waterfalls. The water features are rimmed by slopes carefully planted with pines, rhododendrons, azaleas, and trailing cotoneasters that are pruned and trained to reveal their sculptural qualities.

Fujitaro Kubota's design work for Bloedel Reserve's Japanese Garden and his contributions to the early designs of Washington Park Arboretum's

Japanese Garden attest to his deep knowledge of traditional principles of Japanese garden design. In his own garden, however, Kubota elected to use only those traditional principles which adapt particularly well to the Pacific Northwest setting.

In the core garden, for instance, the principles of "borrowing" and framing a large view from outside the garden, of careful integration of formal and informal areas in the garden, and of an exquisite balancing of water, rock, and plant features are scrupulously followed. Yet Kubota's careful and appreciative use of regional natives and exotics common to Pacific Northwest gardens—bigleaf maples, sword ferns, and many occidental varieties of pines and firs—add a New World shagginess and ranginess to the scene.

Fine stands of Japanese red and black pines, weeping Eastern white pine, *Rhododendron* 'Britannia,' and other trees and shrubs, many of them originally nursery stock that was left to grow to maturity, tie the formal and informal areas of the garden together. A large bamboo grove near the stream at the bottom of the boundary ravine includes yellow-groove (*Phyllostachys aureosulcata*) and the rare black-groove (*P. nigra* 'meijiro').

BEST TIMES TO VIEW

From April to mid-June rhododendrons, azaleas, and iris bloom; from late September to early November Japanese maples, dogwoods, and stands of euonymus provide fine fall color. The textures and barks of conifers are especially attractive in winter.

Renton Ave S and 55th Ave S. Mailing address: Kubota Gardens Foundation, P.O. Box 12646, Seattle, WA 98111-4646, (206) 684-4584. Daily, dawn to dusk. (The waterfall, which is powered by a pump, flows only when staff are present: Apr–Oct, daily until 3:30; Nov–Mar, weekdays until 3:30.) From downtown Seattle, travel south on I-5, take Albro-Swift exit (exit 161), cross over freeway via the bridge, and turn right on Swift; continue on Swift, which becomes Myrtle and then Othello; turn right onto Martin Luther King Jr. Way, and then angle almost immediately left onto Renton Ave S. Travel on Renton Ave S right to to 55th St S, turn right, and park in the small graveled area on the right, about halfway down the block.

Guided tours by appointment; no restrooms; limited wheelchair access; waterproof footgear necessary in wet weather; free.

Medicinal Herb Garden
SEATTLE

For thousands of years our ancestors used curative plants, and collections of medicinal herbs were among the earliest gardens ever planted. Today's medicinal herb gardens thus have historical and botanic significance for visitors; it is an added treat that such collections, with their billowing herbs and shrubs planted in rectangular beds, also make attractive destination gardens.

The University of Washington's Medicinal Herb Garden was established in 1911 on a 1-acre site. At its peak, during World War II, it covered 8 acres and featured almost 850 species of plants representing all corners of the earth. By the early 1960s the gardens had shrunk to their present 2 acres due to campus building expansions, and for the next 20 years the site was neglected and overgrown.

Today a group of volunteers, Friends of the Medicinal Herb Garden, assist the University's Botany Department in upgrading and maintaining several garden rooms filled with beds of medicinal herbs and shrubs. The collection features almost 600 species, many of them grown from seed gathered worldwide, making it the largest such garden in North and South America. Be sure to visit Cascara Circle, a circular garden area featuring a raised pool and delightful wooden monkeys perched on twin pillars near the entryway. The gardens reach their peak of bloom in early summer.

University of Washington campus, on Stevens Way across from the Botany greenhouse. Mailing address: Friends of the Medicinal Herb Garden, Botany Department KB-15, University of Washington, Seattle, WA 98195, (206) 543-1126. Daily during daylight hours. From I-5, take NE 45th St exit (exit 169) and travel east to UW campus.

Labels; self-guiding brochure; free guided tours second and fourth Suns at noon during the growing season; tours at other times by arrangement for a small fee; campus restrooms; limited wheelchair access; free.

Parsons Gardens
SEATTLE

This half-acre gem originally was private, and it preserves a family garden's well-cherished, intimate atmosphere even though it has been open to the public under the aegis of the Seattle Parks and Recreation Department since 1956. Although it is sited across the street from a point with sweeping views of Puget Sound, the garden itself feels enclosed and secluded. The emphasis is on plants rather than on a complex landscape design; trees, shrubs, perennials, and groundcovers weave together in an informal planting scheme that emphasizes year-round color and bloom. Visitors on a mild late-February day, for instance, will find camellias, pieris, hellebores, crocuses, daffodils, and a wonderful old cornelian cherry (*Cornus mas*) in bloom, while in May the garden hits its peak with flowering kolkwitzias, dogwoods, wisteria, lilacs, columbines, meconopsis, violets, and foxgloves. Summer brings on hybrid tea roses, alstroemeria, clumps of yellow loosestrife standing 6 feet tall, and Japanese anemones; August is a good time to visit when glossy-leaved abelias and a rare-in-Seattle chaste tree (*Vitex agnus-castus*) reach their peak of bloom.

7th Ave W and W Highland Dr, (206) 684-4075. Daily, year-round, during daylight hours. From downtown Seattle, take Queen Anne Ave N to W Highland Dr and travel west to 7th Ave W.

No restrooms; some wheelchair access; free.

Tilth and Good Shepherd Demonstration Gardens

SEATTLE

The Seattle Tilth Association is a volunteer organization dedicated to organic gardening, urban ecology, composting, and recycling. Although most of the site's demonstration gardens feature organically grown vegetables and herbs, some splendid perennial borders are going in around the Good Shepherd Center grounds and parking lots. Especially noteworthy is a spacious drought-tolerant bed near the Tilth veggie patches, featuring ornamental herbs and perennials that are at their peak in midsummer.

4649 Sunnyside Ave N, Seattle, WA 98103, (206) 633-0451. Daily during daylight hours. From I-5, take NE 45th St exit (exit 169), travel west on NE 45th St to Sunnyside Ave N and turn right.

Labels; programs; classes; plant sales; restrooms; limited wheelchair access; free.

Volunteer Park Conservatory
SEATTLE

 This glass-and-iron conservatory, set among the wide lawns and towering trees of one of Seattle's finest old parks on Capitol Hill, was built in 1912. Designed after Victorian London's famous Crystal Palace, the glass building was manufactured in New York, shipped in pieces to Seattle, then assembled on site. The conservatory was a late addition to a formal enclave of terraces, bronze statues, pergolas, and grand viewing concourse that the Olmsted Brothers, the nation's leading firm of landscape architects, had designed in a 1904 master plan for Volunteer Park. Many of the features called for in the Olmsted plan either were never built or disappeared over time. The conservatory remained, but was in shaky condition by the late 1970s.

That's when a citizen's group, the Friends of the Conservatory, began working with the Seattle Parks and Recreation Department, which administers the conservatory, to fund a complete renovation of the structure. The project, completed in 1985, reused the original panes of glass whenever practicable. Currently under consideration are proposals to double the display areas, add a gift shop, and provide better facilities for educational programs and handicapped visitors. Funds for these projects would be raised through private donations.

The conservatory features five rooms, each with a distinctive climatic zone geared to the plants it displays. The central room contains palms, banana plants, heliconias, and gingers, whose dramatic foliage acts as a backdrop to a well-known collection of species and hybrid orchids. The orchids, which include some rare varieties of old hybrids sought after by conservatories and private collectors from around the world, put on their finest period of bloom during the fall to early winter.

The east wing houses a large collection of cacti and succulents, whose convoluted, compacted, and bewhiskered shapes fascinate children. This collection flowers in February, March, and April.

The conservatory's seasonal display room contains a permanent collection of foliage plants, such as peperomias, begonias, and coleus. The conservatory staff uses this room for floral displays throughout the year.

West of the main entrance is a fern house that features a koi-filled pond gouged out of lava rock and a display of sago palms (already ancient when dinosaurs roamed the jungles) and giant Mexican monsteras. The emphasis in this house is on texture and form, with a variety of tropical and hardy ferns spreading their fringed wings against the rocky backdrop.

The westernmost room contains one of the finest collections of bromeliads under glass on the West Coast. Many varieties of bromeliads are epiphytes—plants that take their nourishment from the air. Their sword-thin leaves and jewel-toned winter-flowering rosettes are complemented by the thick and shaggy leaves of the staghorn fern collection housed in the same room.

1400 E Galer St, Seattle 98112, (206) 684-4743. May 1–Sept 15, daily 10–7; Sept 16–Apr 30, daily 10–4. From I-5, take Roanoke exit (exit 168 A) east to 10th Ave E; travel south on 10th Ave E (which eventually becomes Broadway Ave E) to Prospect St, turn left, and follow signs to Volunteer Park.
    Park restrooms; limited wheelchair access; free.

Walker Rock Garden
SEATTLE

Mortaring rocks, glass, semiprecious stones, and shells into walls, terraces, and other garden hardscapes is a time-hallowed art. By the 15th century, for instance, Italian gardens featured mysterious stone grottoes whose interiors sparkled with carbuncles, shards of quartz, and even pearls. The Walker Rock Garden, with its stone-studded walls and terraces, miniature mountains carved from red and white lava, glass "lakes," and arching stone towers encrusted with geodes and crushed glass, is an intriguing example of this ancient art form, set down in a traditional West Seattle neighborhood.

Milton and Florence Walker, who built the rock garden in their backyard between 1959 and 1980, used no historical models; instead, they let the site, their imaginations, and the available materials dictate the outcome. The resulting landscape is lively, surprising, and invigorating, as the best folk art often is. The garden holds open house three times each spring; private tours also may be arranged from early April through Labor Day. A donation is suggested. For further information, contact Mrs. Walker at (206) 935-3036.

Washington Park Arboretum
SEATTLE

 At first glance, it looks simply like a tranquil Northwest woodland garden, but Seattle's Washington Park Arboretum actually contains exotic horticultural treasures around every bend in the path, from trees native to New Zealand, Chile, and Japan to rhododendrons and azaleas from China and the Himalayas. With its various plant collections grouped either taxonomically, by natural habitat, or by seasonal bloom, the arboretum documents the rich variety of plants that can flourish in western Washington's mild climate.

SIGNIFICANT FEATURES

- 200 acres featuring woodland glens, naturalistic ponds, wooded slopes, and forest paths
- notable collections of hollies, magnolias, maples, cherries, heaths, and conifers
- specialty gardens, including a marshland, a winter garden, and an elegant Japanese stroll garden

HISTORY

The city of Seattle acquired the land for the present arboretum in 1903, but plans for developing the site took shape only in 1936, when the Parks Department, the University of Washington, and private volunteer groups joined forces in commissioning the Olmsted Brothers, then the nation's premier landscape architecture firm, to create an overall design.

Earlier, the arboretum site had been logged and graded, with large portions of a central ravine (the present-day Azalea Way) flattened for a horse-racing course. The Olmsted plan called for extensive reconfiguration of the land, a task undertaken by several federal work-relief programs in the late 1930s. The WPA, for instance, created Azalea Way's slopes and ravines using hand shovels and spades, and then added 500 railroad cars of compost to the soil by hand. Some of the flowering cherries, dogwoods, rhododendrons, and azaleas planted by the WPA still line Azalea Way today.

The 1936 Olmsted plan also called for the displaying of tree collections in traditional taxonomic groupings; a Japanese garden; alpine gardens at the north end of the arboretum on the present-day marshland Foster Island; and a 10-acre circular rose garden at the arboretum's southwest corner, near Madison Street. Over the next ten years, many of the plan's proposed plant collections were installed, although some were moved in later years to spots with better growing conditions. Other proposed installations, such as the Foster Island alpine gardens and the formal rose gardens near the Madison entrance, were abandoned for more naturalistic landscaping plans.

Today the city of Seattle, the university's Center for Urban Horticulture, and private groups, notably the Arboretum Foundation, continue to develop the arboretum's plant collections and specialty gardens, as well as promote educational and research programs.

THE GARDEN PLAN

Visitors can pick up self-guiding brochures and start their tour at the Graham Visitor Center, a complex that houses offices, meeting rooms, and a gift shop. It features a trellised courtyard garden and handsome iron scroll entry gates designed by Seattle artist George Tsutakawa. The Visitor Center is also the starting place for docent-led tours.

Since 1936 over 5000 native and exotic woody plants have been added to the arboretum, most of them planted in special collections. **The Woodland Garden** displays over 50 varieties of Japanese maples, interplanted with Asian dogwoods (*Cornus kousa*) and other ornamental woodland shrubs and groundcovers that cover shady slopes surrounding a stream and naturalistic ponds. Nearby are **Loderi Valley,** a ravine featuring hybrid rhododendrons and magnolias, and **Rhododendron Glen,** with species and hybrid rhododendrons.

Some collections are planted in sites that replicate, as closely as possible, their natural growing conditions in the wild. **The Flats,** a wet meadow area that runs parallel to the west edge of Lake Washington Boulevard, features trees able to withstand wet winter soils, including red maples (*Acer rubrum*), swamp cypresses (*Taxodium distichum*), and dawn redwoods (*Metasequoia glyptostroboides*). Various pines and giant sequoias (*Sequoiadendron giganteum*) flourish in a sunny, well-drained site in the northwest sector of the arboretum.

Other collections group plants according to seasonal interest. **Azalea Way,** the long woodland path running east of Lake Washington Boulevard, features spring-flowering azaleas, cherries, and dogwoods, while the **Joseph A. Witt Winter Garden,** just north of the Woodland Garden, displays plants with winter interest, including witch hazels, sasanqua camellias, winter-sweet (*Chimonanthus praecox*), paperbark maples (*Acer griseum*), and a host of winter-flowering perennials.

In addition to exotics, the arboretum hosts extensive collections of labeled native trees, shrubs, and groundcovers.

Foster Island, a wetland featuring such natives as alders (*Alnus rubra*) and cascaras (*Rhamnus purshiana*) mixed with introduced exotics, has floating walkways that allow visitors to view the waterside vegetation and waterfowl close up.

THE JAPANESE GARDEN
SEATTLE

 Although establishing a Japanese garden for the arboretum was discussed as early as 1924, plans got under way only in 1960, when the noted Japanese landscape architect Juki Iida was commissioned to design a 3½-acre stroll garden. Based on the pleasure grounds developed for aristocrats and wealthy merchants in 16th- and 17th-century Japan, stroll gardens are designed to gradually reveal views and featured elements, such as waterfalls or rock groupings, as visitors stroll along twisting garden paths. Gardens designed on the stroll model can make even relatively small sites look spacious because they use the technique of alternating enclosed, intimate vignettes with sweeping views of ponds or hillsides—with some of these latter natural features "borrowed" from landscape lying outside the boundaries of the garden. In the arboretum's stroll garden, a central pond acts as the focus of the landscape, with paths winding around it through plantings of pines, Japanese maples, and a rich palette of ornamental shrubs.

Iida coordinated the work of six additional landscape architects in finalizing plans for the new garden, and then personally supervised its installation during the exceptionally rainy spring of 1960. A volunteer remembers the designer, then a man of 70, as "ever in dark beret and raincoat, with white tennis shoes, meticulously directing the placement of each rock and plant." The plan evokes miniature mountains, valleys, and seas through the skillful manipulation of hardscapes, plants, and water. An authentic teahouse, built in the traditional manner without nails, is enclosed by its own exquisitely detailed garden.

Almost 35 years after its construction, the Japanese garden has reached a graceful maturity; after the exuberant azalea and rhododendron display in mid-spring, the garden settles down to a refined celebration of texture and form for the rest of the year.

BEST TIMES TO VIEW

The arboretum can be visited year-round; stop in at the Graham Visitor Center for a table display of blooms from trees and shrubs currently in flower. Spring is the prime flowering season, when azaleas, rhododendrons, flowering cherries, magnolias, and dogwoods blaze against the surrounding conifers and broad-leafed evergreens. The changing foliage in the Woodland Garden is of special interest in the fall.

Visit the Japanese Garden in early to mid-spring for flowering cherries, azaleas, and wisteria; delicate stands of iris bloom along the edges of the pond in June. October brings exceptionally vibrant color to the Japanese maples around the waterfall and stream near the teahouse.

2300 Arboretum Dr E, Seattle, WA 98112, (206) 543-8800. Arboretum, daily during daylight hours; Graham Visitor Center, weekdays, 10–4, weekends and holidays, 12–4. From I-5, take Madison St exit (exit 164A) travel east on Madison; and turn left onto Lake Washington Blvd E.
    Labels; guided tours; self-guiding brochures; programs; classes; gift shop; restrooms; some wheelchair access; free.

Japanese Garden: *March–Nov, daily from 10 (call Seattle Parks and Recreation Dept, 684-4725, for varying closing times). Self-guiding brochures; guided tours by arrangement; nonparticipatory demonstration of formal tea ceremony third Sun, Apr–Oct, 1:30 and 2; arboretum restrooms; limited wheelchair access; fee.*

Woodland Park Rose Garden
SEATTLE

This 2½-acre garden was established in 1922 by the Seattle Parks and Recreation Department to take advantage of the site's good air circulation, sunny exposure, and rich loam—all of which combine to create excellent growing conditions for roses.

Today 5000 plants representing almost 200 varieties of climbing and shrub roses flourish in an attractive setting that includes a formal raised pool, evergreens and conifers shorn into fat lozenges and cumulus clouds, and, in June, deep beds of spiky delphiniums edging trellises and fences. The garden is a test site for All-America Rose selections.

700 N 50th, Seattle, WA 98103, (206) 684-4880. Daily during daylight hours. From I-5, take NE 50th St exit (exit 169), travel west to Fremont Ave N, turn right, and park in Woodland Park Zoo lot.
    Zoo restrooms; some wheelchair access; free.

Woodland Park Zoological Gardens
SEATTLE

A national leader in the creation of naturalistic animal and plant exhibits, Woodland Park Zoo features simulations of a Southeast Asian forest, an African savannah, a Himalayan mountain slope, and temperate-zone marshes and wetlands. Eventually the zoo plans to establish a total of ten distinct bioclimatic life zones on site, with projects currently under way, including an enclosed 4-acre tropical rain forest and a temperate-zone forest. The grounds also support a collection of bamboos and a compact native plant garden.

5500 Phinney Ave N, Seattle, WA 98103, (206) 684-4800. Nov–Feb, daily 10–4; March, daily 10–5; Apr-Sept, weekdays 10–6, weekends and holidays, 8:30–6; October, daily 10–5. From I-5, take NE 50th St exit (exit 169), travel west to Fremont Ave N, and turn right to parking lot.

Some labels; programs; classes; snack bars; gift shops; restrooms; wheelchair-accessible throughout; fee.

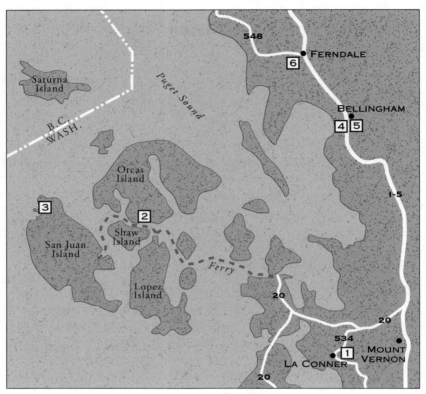

1. La Conner Flats Display Garden, *La Conner*
2. Orcas Hotel Garden, *Orcas Island*
3. Roche Harbor Resort Garden, *San Juan Island*
4. Fairhaven Rose Garden, *Bellingham*
5. Sehome Hill Arboretum, *Bellingham*
6. Tennant Lake Nature Walk/Fragrance Garden/Hovander Homestead, *Ferndale*

Roche Harbor Resort Garden, *San Juan Island*

Northern Washington
La Conner Flats Display Garden
LA CONNER

 This 11-acre garden features seasonal displays of daffodils (March), tulips (April), rhododendrons and azaleas (March through May), roses, perennials, and herbs (summer), and dahlias and chrysanthemums (late summer through fall).

La Conner Flats is a young garden. Its nucleus was originally the private garden of former nursery owners Bob and Marjorie Hart, who expanded the garden considerably before opening it to the public in 1988. Because a significant number of the garden's plantings are new, it has a certain raw quality that may soften in time as the evergreen "bones"—hedges and conifer plantings—grow to maturity.

An old granary on the property has been refurbished into a rustic tearoom where lunches and desserts are served.

1598 Best Rd, Mount Vernon, WA 98273, (206) 466-3190. Daily, Mar–Oct, 10–6. From I-5, take exit 230 (Hwy 20) west 5 miles to Best Rd; drive south on Best Rd for 2 miles.
   Some labels; restaurant; restrooms; limited wheelchair access; fee.

Orcas Hotel Garden
ORCAS ISLAND

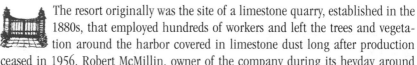 When picturesque Orcas Hotel was built at the turn of the century, extensive gardens were installed around its main building. Period photographs show a layout that included rock walls, apple trees, and planting beds filled with the most fashionable flowers of the day. Although subsequent owners gradually decreased the size of the grounds to their present half acre, an apple tree and irises planted over 80 years ago continue to flourish today.

In 1985 the garden underwent a major renovation. A rockery built from island limestone and a white picket fence were restored, and a number of native plants were added. With the aid of old photographs as references, plants found in the original garden—wisteria, clematis, and herbs—were reintroduced to the site.

Mailing address: Orcas Hotel, P.O. Box 155, Orcas, WA 98280, (206) 376-4300. Daily during daylight hours. Across from Orcas Island ferry dock.
   Restrooms; limited wheelchair access; free.

Roche Harbor Resort Garden
SAN JUAN ISLAND

The resort originally was the site of a limestone quarry, established in the 1880s, that employed hundreds of workers and left the trees and vegetation around the harbor covered in limestone dust long after production ceased in 1956. Robert McMillin, owner of the company during its heyday around the turn of the century, built his family an opulent Victorian gable-and-gingerbread home on the shore. The walkways of its small but pretty garden were made of cobblelike bricks that had originally been used in the limestone kilns.

The McMillin house is now the Roche Harbor Restaurant, and visitors may stroll the pleasant old garden, with its trellises, white picket fence, and old-fashioned perennial borders. A trail from the resort leads through the woods above the harbor to the site of the McMillin family mausoleum—a wonderfully romantic woodland glen where stone pillars encircle rugged slabs of limestone that contain the ashes of family members.

Mailing address: Roche Harbor Resort, P.O. Box 4001, Roche Harbor, WA 98250, (206) 378-2155. Daily during daylight hours. From Friday Harbor ferry terminal, take Spring St 2 blocks to 2nd St, turn right and follow 2nd for 0.3 mile; turn right to Tucker Ave and travel 9 miles (the name changes to Roche Harbor Rd) to the end of the road.
Restrooms; free.

Fairhaven Rose Garden
BELLINGHAM

 This 1-acre All-America Rose Selection garden, part of the Olmsted Brothers–designed Fairhaven Park, features Victorian-style wood trellises and arbors as intricate as spider webs, set among rose beds planted with over 100 varieties of hybrid teas, floribundas, and grandifloras. A kiosk in the center of the garden lists the rose varieties currently displayed, along with their locations in the beds.

107 Chuckanut Dr, Bellingham, WA 98225, (206) 676-6985 (Bellingham City Parks and Recreation Department). Daily during daylight hours. From I-5, take Bellingham exit 250, drive west on Old Fairhaven Pkwy to 12th St, and turn left (south); the garden is on the right, immediately after 12th St turns into Chuckanut Dr.
Some labels; no restrooms; some wheelchair access; free.

Sehome Hill Arboretum
BELLINGHAM

 This 165-acre native plant preserve caps Sehome Hill, which also features dramatic views of Bellingham Bay from several points along its network of walking trails. Sehome Hill fell into private hands as early as 1855, but its rugged topography precluded any building on the site. Logging and several fires destroyed the original old growth between 1870 and 1900; however, much of the forest that visitors see today remains intact from the turn of the century.

In 1974 the city of Bellingham and Western Washington University, now its prime owners, formally dedicated Sehome Hill as a jointly managed arboretum for native plants. Visitors can see Douglas firs, bigleaf maples, western hemlocks, sword ferns, and various native groundcovers and mosses.

Western Washington University campus, Bellingham, WA 98225; no phone. Daily 6–10. From I-5, take exit 252, travel west on Bill McDonald Parkway, and look for signs to arboretum on right.
   Campus restrooms; limited wheelchair access; free.

Tennant Lake Nature Walk/ Fragrance Garden/Hovander Homestead
FERNDALE

 Cattails and coriander, duckweed and dill—visitors can savor some unusual plant combinations when they combine a walk along Tennant Lake's nature loop with a stroll through the nearby Fragrance Garden. The nature loop's half-mile boardwalk skirts the southern shore of the lake and then skims a marsh and swamp; native rushes, willows, and skunk cabbages are abundant, and visitors might glimpse muskrats, beavers, and hawks. The park is managed by the Whatcom County Parks and Recreation Department, which also maintains an interpretive center—a renovated pioneer farmhouse with some lovely perennial borders at the head of the trail.

Just outside the interpretive center is the exceptionally attractive **Fragrance Garden,** installed by the Whatcom County Parks and Recreation Advisory Board and a consortium of local garden clubs. Serpentine planting beds bursting with scented herbs and perennials wind along a central pathway designed for easy access by wheelchair users and the visually impaired. On a sultry August day after a short but drenching rain, visitors may find themselves moved to dive into the garden as if it were a deep bowl of damply pungent potpourri.

A nature trail takes visitors on a pleasant 20-minute walk through fields to the **Hovander Homestead,** a turn-of-the-century pioneer home and garden, also managed by the Whatcom County Parks and Recreation Department, with assistance from local Master Gardeners. The Homestead includes farm animals, displays of antique farm equipment, and a viewing tower overlooking the Nooksack River. Gardeners will find the compact fruit, herb, and vegetable gardens especially interesting. A fine dahlia display in beds near the house begins in late summer.

5299 Nielsen Rd, Ferndale, WA 98248, (206) 384-3444. Tennant Lake Nature Walk: daily during daylight hours. Fragrance Garden: daily,

8:30–dusk. Hovander Homestead gardens: daily during daylight hours. From I-5, take exit 262 (Ferndale exit), travel west ½ mile, turn left just past the railroad underpass, and follow signs to Tennant Lake. Visitors can also drive directly to the Hovander Homestead.

Some labels; self-guiding brochures; visitors' center; programs; classes; picnic facilities; restrooms; some wheelchair access; free (parking fee at Hovander Homestead for out-of-county visitors).

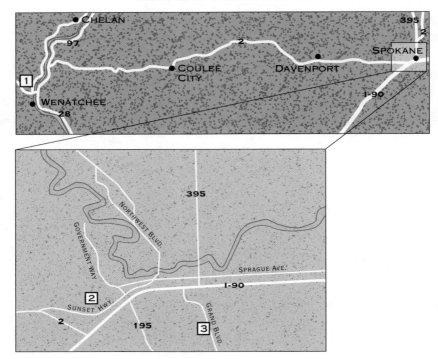

EASTERN WASHINGTON

Ohme Gardens, *Wenatchee*

EASTERN WASHINGTON

Ohme Gardens

WENATCHEE

Visitors to 9-acre Ohme Gardens may feel as though they've stepped into a stage set for *The Sound of Music*—alpine meadows thick with gold and purple groundcovers sweep down rocky outcroppings to forest glens and ice-clear mountain ponds. Under streaming sunlight and an enamel-blue sky, clusters of conifers lead the eye beyond the garden's ridges and ravines to panoramic views of a river flowing through monumental hills and valleys. Impossibly perfect and, at the same time, perfectly natural, this garden is a magical melding of the wild and the subtly contrived.

Rough-and-tumble in spirit yet manicured in appearance, Ohme Gardens creates an artful interpretation of the surrounding landscape (the sere eastern foothills of the Cascade Mountains in central Washington) by combining stony upland terrain with an innovative palette of native and exotic plants, one that is aesthetically pleasing and horticulturally right for the site conditions. The result is one of the masterwork public gardens of the United States.

SIGNIFICANT FEATURES
- a superb garden plan incorporating the design elements of rock, water, and hillside topography
- paths of native stone that wander up and down the garden hillsides, linking together ponds, meadows, rock outcroppings, and viewing points
- dramatic views of the Wenatchee Valley, the Cascade Mountains, and the Columbia River

HISTORY
In 1929 Wenatchee Valley orchardists Herman and Ruth Ohme decided to transform a rocky bluff on their property into a private alpine oasis. For the next ten years, during their leisure hours, the Ohmes hauled tons of native granite, basalt, and sedimentary stones up the slopes of the garden by mule, creating more outcrops and building a network of paths and steps throughout the site. They also planted hundreds of native conifers, collected as seedlings from the nearby mountains and foothills, between the rock outcrops and paths. During these first years, a cumbersome arrangement of hoses and sprinkler heads brought water to the site.

In 1939 the Ohmes decided to turn their full attention to developing the garden. Renting their orchards to tenant farmers, they opened the garden to the public and at the same time embarked on a further series of improvements that were to occupy them for the next several decades. During this period the Ohmes dug vast underground webs of irrigation piping into the hillside and introduced a variety of groundcovers to act as the garden floor. They also constructed ponds, austerely beautiful stone benches, and a stonework lookout tower with views out over the hills and valleys beyond.

A second generation of Ohmes, Gordon and Carol, took formal charge of the garden between the early 1970s and 1991. Under their meticulous care the garden flourished and expanded. But over time the workload became increasingly onerous, and in late 1991 the Ohmes sold the property to the Washington State Parks Commission with the proviso that it remain a garden in perpetuity. Gordon and Carol Ohme continue to advise the garden's present state-appointed administrator/caretaker, Joe Mullen, on maintenance and renovation. Ruth Ohme, now in her energetic eighties, still enjoys visiting the garden often—after all, she tended it daily as a labor of love for well over 60 years.

THE GARDEN PLAN

Ohme Gardens makes good use of the hollows, ridges, outcrops, and sloping meadows found naturally in mountain foothills. These features are studded with an elegant overlay of stone paths and steps that carry visitors through a range of garden experiences. Enclosed forest glades give way to open meadows with sweeping views. These are, in turn, succeeded by steep, stony ridges that lead to sheltered ravines with ponds nestled in their deepest hollows. Each of these garden features is set off by a variety of carefully selected conifers and groundcovers.

Thickets of Pacific Northwest native conifers such as Western red cedars (*Thuja plicata*), hemlocks (both *Tsuga heterophylla* and *T. mertensiana*), Pacific silver firs (*Abies amabilis*), and Engelmann spruce (*Picea engelmanii*) provide an evergreen backbone for the garden and also create cool, shaded microenvironments for the ferns, trilliums, creeping mahonias, and hostas that serve as their understory.

The clumped conifers border brilliantly sunny alpine meadows of pink phlox (*P. subulata* 'Nelsonii'), basket-of-gold (*Aurinia saxatilis*), blue bugleweed (*Ajuga pyramidalis*), thrift (*Armeria maritima*), periwinkle (*Vinca minor*), and white rock cress (*Arabis caucasia*). Dwarf creeping junipers, eight different thymes, sedums, and saxifrages hug the stony outcrops, while ferns and hostas rim the shaded ravines and ponds.

One feature that can always be enjoyed at Ohme Gardens is the sheer perfection of its maintenance. Usually the garden visitor notices maintenance only in its absence, but Ohme Gardens elevates upkeep to a fine art. During her tenure as caretaker, Ruth Ohme could be seen early most mornings stooped over one stretch or another of the garden's miles of grass and groundcover borders, grooming its edges with hand clippers the size of pinking shears. And each level grassy area carved into the hillside is kept shorn by its own lawnmower, kept parked behind a nearby rock. Joe Mullen plans to uphold the Ohme family's standards: "I'm not a gardener," he explains cheerfully, "I'm a manicurist."

Ohme Gardens' eclectic combination of native and exotic plants is unconventional, even eccentric, but it works. In this slightly surreal yet wholly engaging landscape, a unique sensibility has transmuted the many decorative aspects of mountain terrain and its plant life into a new and unique style of garden.

BEST TIMES TO VIEW

The meadow groundcovers usually reach their height of bloom during the last two weeks of April and the first week of May. The thymes also flower in May, followed by thrifts and sedums in June. In summer and fall, trees and groundcovers with widely contrasting textures ring a thousand changes on the color green.

3327 Ohme Rd, Wenatchee, WA 98801, (509) 662-5785. April 15–Memorial Day, daily 9–6; Memorial Day–Labor Day, daily 9–7; Labor Day–Oct 14, daily 9–6. Closed Oct 15–Apr 14. From Wenatchee, take US 97 north for 3 miles to where it joins Hwy 2 and follow signs.

Restrooms; drinking fountain; no wheelchair access; flat, sturdy shoes a must; sun protection desirable; fee.

John A. Finch Arboretum
SPOKANE

 This mile-long finger of an arboretum stretching along the banks of Garden Springs Creek was established by the Spokane Parks Department at the same time work began on Manito Park, although systematic planting of trees and shrubs began here only in 1949. Today the 65-acre arboretum displays over 600 species and varieties of woody plants, with wild areas of native plants alternating with collections of conifers, maples, hawthorns, and flowering shrubs. Flowering rhododendrons, lilacs, and crabapples make mid-spring a prime time for visiting.

W 3404 Woodland Blvd, Spokane, WA 99201, (509) 625-6655. Daily during daylight hours. From downtown Spokane, go west on 2nd Ave to Sunset Hwy (I-90 Business Route) and continue west on Sunset past Government Way; look for signs to arboretum entry on left.

Some labels, including braille; self-guiding brochure; visitors' center; no restrooms; limited wheelchair access; free.

Manito Park and Botanical Gardens
SPOKANE

 The rolling green lawns and towering shade trees of Manito Park and Botanical Gardens display an air of lavish comfort reminiscent of the Edwardian era in which they were planted. Established by the Spokane

Park Board between 1907 and 1913, Manito offers a wide array of horticultural delights, from rose beds and indoor tropical plants to topiaries, fountains, and a butterfly garden. The spacious landscape and the leisured atmosphere at Manito make it easy to imagine oneself strolling along its paths in high-buttoned boots and a feathered hat some sunny Sunday afternoon in 1910, listening to the decorous toots and honks of a uniformed brass band.

SIGNIFICANT FEATURES
- a 90-acre campus designed by the Olmsted Brothers
- perennial gardens, a conservatory, rose gardens, a Japanese garden, an extensive lilac collection, and a formal garden with topiaries, a fountain, and geometric beds of annuals

HISTORY
During the 1890s, the Manito site served as a stop on the city trolley line, and it boasted a small zoo and some picnic areas. When the Spokane Park Board acquired the property in 1907, it commissioned the Olmsted Brothers to lay out the park and its major garden areas. Manito's development coincided with a period of bustling prosperity for Spokane, and many of the city's businessmen vied in contributing land, buildings, and construction funds to the project. By 1913 the park's major features had been established; the only significant later addition, the Spokane Nishinomiya Japanese Garden, was completed in 1974.

THE GARDEN PLAN
Entering Manito from Park Drive off Grand Boulevard, visitors drive through a cool, expansive sweep of trees and lawns where a duck pond, picnic tables, and the lilac collection are sited.

Just beyond the picnic area lies the **Joel E. Ferris Perennial Gardens,** a 3-acre enclave of free-form sun and shade perennial borders set in a grassy lawn. The borders are designed to flower from spring through early autumn; in a mid-August visit the sunny beds may display "cool" areas of silver and blue-flowering plants alternating with "hot" beds of scarlet dahlias and purple coneflowers. A handsome shade border on a rocky slope features trollius, daylilies, variegated hostas, and Japanese anemones framed by clipped yews. Nearby, a small, labeled hummingbird and butterfly garden is centered around a stone birdbath.

Rose Hill, a 4-acre hill overlooking the perennial gardens, is bordered by a wonderful stone retaining wall spilling over with basket-of-gold alyssum, candytuft, sedums, and phlox. The rose garden, a cooperative project of the Spokane Rose Society and the Spokane Parks Department, features neat rows of labeled hybrid teas (over 150 varieties) and some informal beds on a rocky outcrop planted in bush roses, daylilies, and low conifers. Collections of old-fashioned and miniature roses are also on view.

Gaiser Conservatory features unusually attractive collections of tropical plants, cactus, and flowering annuals, displayed in a cool, watery setting that makes for a refreshing stop on a hot summer day.

Across from the main entry to the conservatory, a flight of steps leads visitors down into **Duncan Garden,** a 3-acre formal garden where clipped shrubs shaped like lollipops march along the borders and geometric beds of annuals line up at attention along gravel paths. Long borders of rangy phlox and cosmos provide informal touches in this otherwise perfectly symmetrical landscape, while a white granite fountain in the center of the garden adds the subtly anarchic presence of water to the scene.

The latest addition to the park is **Spokane Nishinomiya Japanese Garden.** Built to honor the friendship between Spokane and its Japanese sister city Nishinomiya, the garden features striking stone and metal lanterns imported from Japan, as well as a handsome waterfall, stream, and rock complex. The garden's plantings seem less successful than its hardscapes, possibly because Spokane's climate requires some use of plants not traditionally associated with Japanese gardens.

BEST TIMES TO VIEW

The perennial gardens start their show in spring with bulbs and primroses and continue until fall with chrysanthemums and dahlias. The lilac collection usually peaks in the second or third week in May, when the city sponsors a Lilac Festival. Rose Hill blooms from the end of June through frost. Duncan Garden is in bloom from May until early October, although its most impressive season runs from mid-July on.

Between Grand Blvd and Bernard St, extending from 17th Ave to 25th Ave. Mailing address: Spokane Parks Department, 4 W 21st Ave, Spokane, WA 99203, (509) 456-4331. Park: daily year-round, 8–dusk. Gaiser Conservatory: daily except Christmas and New Year's Day, 8–dusk. Japanese Garden: April 1–Oct 31, daily 8–dusk. From I-90 traveling east, take Maple St exit and travel south on Maple St to 21st Ave; turn left and follow signs.

Some labels; self-guiding brochures; restrooms; wheelchair-accessible; free.

BRITISH COLUMBIA

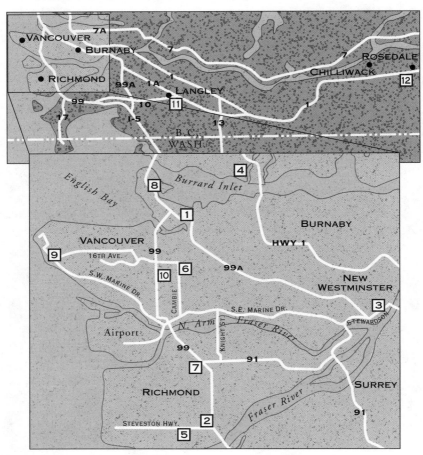

1. Dr. Sun Yat-Sen Classical Chinese Garden, *Vancouver*
2. Fantasy Garden World, *Richmond*
3. Japanese Friendship Garden, *New Westminster*
4. Park & Tilford Gardens, *North Vancouver*
5. Penjing Collection at the International Buddhist Society Temple, *Richmond*
6. Queen Elizabeth Park and Bloedel Conservatory, *Vancouver*
7. Richmond Nature Park, *Richmond*
8. Stanley Park Rose Garden, *Vancouver*
9. University of British Columbia Botanical Garden and Nitobe Memorial Garden, *Vancouver*
10. VanDusen Botanical Garden, *Vancouver*
11. Sendall Gardens, *Langley*
12. Minter Gardens, *Rosedale*

Dr. Sun Yat-Sen Classical Chinese Garden, *Vancouver*

VANCOUVER AND MAINLAND
Dr. Sun Yat-Sen Classical Chinese Garden
VANCOUVER

Lush is the misty grass to the west of the golden pavilion
Tall bamboos shade the door
And plum trees line the garden path. . . .
                    —Tai Fu-Ku (b. 1167)

Spring colors fill the garden, but cannot be contained–
One spray of red almond blossoms peeks over
The whitewashed wall. . . .
                    —Liu Chi (1311–1375)

111

Perhaps the most exotic public garden on the West Coast, and certainly its most exquisite, this classical Chinese garden and its complex of corridors and courtyards may remind visitors of an intricately chambered jewel box. Heaped with delicate horticultural and manmade treasures, it demonstrates why the Chinese have considered the making of gardens a major art form for 20 centuries.

SIGNIFICANT FEATURES

- an outdoor classical Chinese garden in the Ming style
- superb garden structures displaying carved wood screens and roof tiles handmade by Chinese artisans
- an extensive collection of taihu rocks

HISTORY

The Dr. Sun Yat-Sen Classical Chinese Garden was built in 1986 as a joint project between Vancouver and its Chinese sister city Suzhou, which has been famed for over 700 years for its skilled garden designers and exquisite gardens. The Canadian and Chinese governments and private donations funded the $5.5-million construction; gate receipts and fundraising activities support current garden operations. A team of 52 Suzhou artisans spent a year building the 2½-acre complex, which covers most of a city block in the heart of Vancouver's Chinatown.

The garden complex is composed of two areas, each with a separate entrance. The inner **Classical Garden** features a series of elaborate walkways, bridges, carved screen windows, pagodas, and courtyards set off by delicate specimen plants. The outer **Park** is joined to the Classical Garden by a shared wall studded with screened windows that "leak" views between the two areas. The Park is more naturalistic in design than the Classical Garden, with fewer garden structures and more plants, including natives of both China and the Northwest.

Chinese gardens are unfamiliar to most Western gardeners, even Pacific Northwesterners who pride themselves on a growing appreciation of their Pacific Rim neighbor's rich artistic heritage. Yet the tradition of making gardens is ancient, complex, and of central importance in Chinese society. For 2000 years emperors, sages, and scholars spent their best energies making gardens that express the relationship of humans to the divine order, to nature, and to each other.

Quite apart from their spiritual significance, however, Chinese gardens are exquisite works of art, balancing plants and constructed features in subtle relationships that continue to reward attentive study and repeated visits.

As with any fertile art form, numerous schools and styles of Chinese garden design have developed over the centuries. The Dr. Sun Yat-Sen Classical Garden is an example of the Ming school—a style developed by scholars, landowners, and rich merchants during the Ming dynasty (1368–1644) that typically displays sophisticated designs, rare specimen plants, and elaborate garden buildings.

THE GARDEN PLAN

Visitors entering the main courtyard of the Classical Garden encounter a "false mountain" of *taihu* rocks lying in tumbled heaps around a central pond of jade-green water. Taihu rocks are limestone formations dragged from the depths of Lake Tai, near Suzhou in eastern China. Over the course of the centuries, the lake's turbulent, silty waters have carved the rock into fantastic shapes. Washed in shades of gray and white, with gouged and knotted surfaces, taihu rocks look like billowing storm clouds frozen in an instant of time. Highly prized by Chinese garden designers for more than a thousand years, taihu rocks are rarely sent outside of mainland China.

An elegant viewing pavilion, or *t'ing,* perches on the taihu rocks, its lacquered vermilion columns supporting a tiled roof that seems to soar against the squared-off sky above the courtyard walls. The courtyard floor is made of rounded pebbles and broken bits of pottery (these last thriftily shipped from China in enormous crates) set in elaborate designs in concrete. Visitors may find that the courtyard floor is a sensory experience all by itself, when its raised designs massage their feet in ways that at first startle and then gratify as they cross it to a covered walkway nearby.

The walkway skirts the central courtyard and, where it crosses an arm of the central pond, leads into a **Water Pavilion** that is set off from the rest of the courtyard by intricately carved wood screens. These were made by Suzhou artisans using hand tools identical to those their ancestors developed more than five centuries ago.

Stopping to admire the lacy reflection of the screens on the water's surface below, visitors gradually realize that this delicate effect is repeated by the play of sunlight through screened windows set in whitewashed walls behind them. Looking out into the courtyard, they notice the shadows bamboos cast against white walls, the points of sunlight glinting off fluttering leaves, and the continuous wash of light and shadows over the taihu rocks.

At other times in the day, the quality of the light in the Classical Garden changes. Brilliantly clear, it seems to make the dappled gray rocks, charcoal-colored roof tiles, vermilion lacquered fences, and jade-green water glow against the whitewashed walls that surround them. Now the clear light and white walls turn the courtyard into an outdoor art gallery, in which the specimen plants, rocks, and garden structures serve as carefully placed works of art.

Continuing along the walkway, visitors enter the **Scholar's Study,** a small enclosure just off the main courtyard that features plants, a pavilion, and rock sculptures on a refined and delicate scale. The austere vignettes in the Scholar's Study may seem as soothing as sips of green tea to visitors still reeling from the strong wine of the main courtyard.

Plants often are used sparingly in Ming gardens, serving as accents or harmonizers between garden structures. In the main, however, plants are selected for their symbolic significance and because of the interest their forms and textures can bring to the overall composition. Each type of plant in the Classical Garden symbolizes a different but complementary virtue. Bamboo represents flexibility and resilience; pines, strength; bananas, learning; and winter flowering plums, hope.

Because few plants are used in the Classical Garden, each one is choice. For pines and winter plums, the Suzhou designers wanted mature specimens, whose twisting trunks and raised roots would contribute an atmosphere of characterful age to the garden's composition. Several varieties of camellias and azaleas planted in the main courtyard offer year-round interest, as well as scarlet and pink blooms that seem to glow in the pearly light of spring.

The outer Park is planted more lushly and informally, with narrow paths wandering through thick stands of bamboos, pines, and flowering shrubs. On hot summer days, the *t'ing* that extends over the park's central pond provides a cool and breezy point from which to view the water lilies and koi below.

BEST TIMES TO VIEW

The Classical Garden is an all-weather garden. The covered walkways and viewing pavilions permit visits even in downpours, when raindrops fall in lacy patterns from specially contoured roof tiles into the pond below. The Pacific Northwest's occasional snowfall highlights the garden's delicate lines and patterns; the Chinese believe bamboo is viewed to its best advantage under a light cover of snow.

578 Carrall St (downtown Vancouver in Chinatown, next to the Chinese

Cultural Center), Vancouver, BC V6B 2J8, (604) 662-3207. May–Sept, daily 10–8; Oct–Apr, daily 10–4:30.

Some labels in Park, no labels in Classical Garden; self-guiding brochures; guided tours; group tours by arrangement; private rentals available; programs; gift shop; restrooms; some wheelchair access; flat shoes recommended for touring the Classical Garden; free admission to Park, fee for Classical Garden.

Fantasy Garden World
RICHMOND

 Visitors follow mazelike paths through an Olde Worlde Village (20 restaurants and gift shops staffed by dirndled peasants) to reach the entry of Fantasy Garden World. Inside, the 12 acres of display areas comprise numerous beds of annuals, a formal rose garden, a collection of plants mentioned in the Bible accompanied by life-sized statues of biblical personages, a hanging fuchsia garden, and a spacious conservatory. Other attractions include a carillon bell tower, aviaries, and a petting zoo for children and like-minded adults. A Christmas light show runs from the first week of December through the first week of January; the spring tulip display starts in mid-March.

10800 No. 5 Road, Richmond, BC V7A 4E5, (604) 277-7777. Daily, except Christmas Day, 9–dusk. From downtown Vancouver, take Hwy 99 south to Steveston Highway exit, turn west at end of exit ramp, and follow signs.
 Gift shops; restaurants; restrooms; wheelchair-accessible; fee.

Japanese Friendship Garden
NEW WESTMINSTER

This 2½-acre site was designed to honor the gardening traditions of New Westminster's Japanese sister city, Moriguchi. To that end, fir trees, pieris, rhododendrons, flowering cherry trees, and other plants suitable to both Japanese gardens and naturalistic West Coast gardens have been combined in an informal planting scheme. The most interesting part of the site, from a design point of view, centers on four waterfalls, connected by a stream, that cascade down a gentle slope. The design flows from this lyrical central garden into the more prosaic surrounding park area so unobtrusively yet definitively that it may inspire speculation on precisely what differentiates a garden from a park.

Standing at the topmost waterfall, the visitor can see how the plants are used here determines whether they are considered part of the garden area or part of the park, just as how words are used determines whether they are poetry or prose. For instance, in contrast to the park area's somewhat utilitarian arrangement of trees, shrubs, and lawn, the garden area displays plants in a rhythmic, densely textured pattern—one in which the plants play off each other and the nearby water features to achieve a design whose whole equals more than the sum of its parts. And, like stanzas in a poem, the waterfalls work in sequence to develop the overall theme or garden design. (Because this design works well in the landscape, it is easy to over-look the garden's minor flaws, such as the obtrusive concrete foundations of the stream and pools.) The best times to view the garden are in spring, when the Yoshino cherries bloom, and in high summer, when the bamboo and gunnera droop at their most lush over the ponds.

Adjacent to New Westminster Town Hall; no phone. Daily during daylight hours. From downtown Vancouver, take Main St south and turn left onto Kingsway (Hwy 1A/99A); continue east on the highway about 11.2 kilometers (about 7 miles) to the New Westminster city limits, where it becomes 12th St; continue on 12th St about 1.6 kilometers (about 1 mile) and turn left onto Royal Ave. The park is about 0.8 kilometer (about 0.5 mile) farther on the left.
   No restrooms; some wheelchair access; free.

Park & Tilford Gardens
NORTH VANCOUVER

Like the Dr. Sun Yat-Sen Classical Chinese Garden, the Park & Tilford Gardens stand as a noteworthy example of how an elaborate garden design can be successfully executed within a small space. Featuring eight separate garden rooms on a scant 2½ acres, the Park & Tilford Gardens are an elegant horticultural bonbon, one that visitors can savor bite by delectable bite as they stroll through the various garden areas, each complete with its own distinctive style, hardscape, and plant palette.

SIGNIFICANT FEATURES
   - an intricate, yet flowing garden design
   - elegant hardscapes appropriate to each garden room's style

HISTORY
   The gardens were established in 1968 as the grounds surrounding a North Vancouver distillery; they quickly achieved regional prominence because of

their fine collections of magnolias, greenhouse bromeliads, and rare herbaceous perennials. When the distillery closed in 1984, the gardens became derelict, but the merchants in the adjacent shopping center funded a major renovation, completed in 1989. The gardens are maintained by a small full-time staff with the help of local horticultural students. The site is sandwiched between a busy road, the shopping center, and a railway, but despite the background din it is well worth a leisurely visit.

THE GARDEN PLAN

Entering through the street gate, visitors encounter the **Rose Garden,** a formal rectangle bordered by clipped evergreens. Raised beds are filled with 24 varieties of hybrid teas and other shrub roses. During high summer the feet of the rose bushes may be covered in masses of catmint (*Nepeta mussinii*), whose cascading lavender blooms also soften the hard edges of the raised beds with a cool, hazy froth. The fountain and tiled pool at the center of the Rose Garden add a formal finishing touch.

A wrought-iron pergola half buried in climbing roses and wisteria marks the end of the Rose Garden; beyond it lies the small **Herb Garden** planted around a simple circular terrace. One year in late August a sharp-eyed visitor would have discovered, in a sunny sheltered spot between the Herb Garden and the nearby greenhouse, two tender plants seldom seen this far north: a Brazilian native called princess flower (*Tibouchina urvilleana*), with its five-petaled velvety leaves and stunning electric-blue flowers that bloom almost year-round in warm climates, and flannel bush (*Fremontodendron californicum*), a California native with incandescent lemon-yellow blooms. One of Park & Tilford's pleasant surprises is the way such exotics are combined throughout the garden with more standard plants.

The path from the Herb Garden and the greenhouse leads to the **Display Garden,** where a small waterfall trickles into a pool rimmed by lush stands of gunnera, ligularia, and astilbes. This tiny garden area is a fine example of how to establish a distinct style in a small space without making that space feel either tight or oppressive. Beyond the pool are raised beds with seasonal displays of bulbs, annuals, and perennials.

The visitor next enters the **Colonnade,** a series of arches made of stucco, brick, and wood covered with vines and fuchsia baskets that curve around the **White Garden,** a group of raised beds containing plants with silver foliage and/or white blooms. In late summer, clumps of creamy Japanese anemones, paper-white phlox, several varieties of silvery artemisias, *Rudbeckia* 'White Swan,' and felty gray lamb's ears (*Stachys lanata*) make a luminous display. The **Magnolia Garden,** which features unusual specimens from the original garden's collection, borders the White Garden.

Whitewashed walls capped with sky-blue tiles surround the **Oriental Garden,** where the visitor will find a small collection of bamboos, including the seldom-seen *Phyllostachys viridis* 'Robert Young' and some variegated groundcover bamboos.

Beyond lies the pretty **Native Garden** in which mahonia, ferns, salal, *Vancouveria hexandra,* and deciduous huckleberries scramble over snags and the raised roots of towering native firs.

BEST TIMES TO VIEW

Massed bulbs and flowering magnolias are on display February through April; their peak bloom periods usually occur in late March and early April. From June through August is the best time to view roses and perennials, although they often linger through a warm September.

440-333 Brooksbank Ave, North Vancouver, BC V7J 3S8, (604) 984-8200. Daily 9:30–dusk. From downtown Vancouver, follow Hwy 1A/99 through Stanley Park across Lion's Gate Bridge (also called First Narrows Bridge on maps) to North Vancouver; follow Park St east onto Marine Dr and continue straight ahead onto 3rd St, which becomes Cotton Rd; turn left onto Brooksbank.

Labels; restaurants in adjacent shopping center; restrooms available; most paths wheelchair-accessible; traditional Christmas light display every evening between 5 and 9:30 during December; free.

Penjing Collection at the International Buddhist Society Temple

RICHMOND

 The collection of *penjing* (Chinese bonsai) at the International Buddhist Society's Temple on Steveston Highway is displayed in an authentic setting, a lemon-and-celadon-tiled courtyard behind the main temple building. (The temple itself is well worth visiting. Golden lions writhe on its tiled pagoda roofs and 10-foot-high gilt statues of the Buddha glimmer in its shadowed, incense-saturated interior.) To reach the penjing courtyard, walk through the moon gate on the west side of the parking lot, pass through the wide corridor with its clumps of bamboo, and turn left.

The courtyard displays examples of the two main types of penjing. *Tree penjing* feature miniaturized trees and shrubs such as pines, elms, flowering fruit trees, and azaleas planted in ceramic pots, many of which were produced in mainland China; these tree penjing are the forebears of Japanese bonsai.

Rock penjing are abstract compositions made entirely of specimen stones that evoke a whole landscape, such as a mountain chain or a rocky island rising from the sea. The temple's collection features specimens made from both soft and hard rock. A particularly intriguing example made of soft rock is termed *lok kuan*. It is composed of deposits of sea animals formed into ropy swirls that look like bunched roots or tentacles. Another is a "landscape" composed of soft white coral that looks like congealed cream. Among the hard rock displays is a sharply peaked miniature mountain range formed from stalagmites mined in mainland China. The tree and rock penjing are mounted on stands as complex as carved tripods or as simple as cinder blocks—a pleasingly informal and authentic touch.

9160 Steveston Hwy, Richmond, BC V7A 1M5, (604) 274-2822. Daily during daylight hours. From downtown Vancouver, take Hwy 99 south to Steveston Hwy exit and travel west about 1.6 kilometers (about 1 mile); after crossing No. 4 Rd, look to the left for the brightly colored gates of the temple.

Restrooms; wheelchair-accessible; free.

Queen Elizabeth Park
VANCOUVER

This 130-acre park was completed in 1961 to honor Vancouver's 75th anniversary, and it features spectacular 180-degree views of the mountains and inlet that surround the city. Two monumental sunken gardens, carved from an abandoned rock quarry, wind between the park's steep slopes, their floors a fruit salad of bright annuals and perennials set among streams and bridges. The park also features an arboretum of trees and shrubs native to the province and a garden displaying 75 varieties of roses.

W 23rd and Cambie St. Mailing address: Vancouver Board of Parks and Recreation, 2099 Beach Ave, Vancouver, BC V6G IZ4, (604) 872-5513. Daily during daylight hours.
Restrooms; some wheelchair access; free.

BLOEDEL CONSERVATORY
VANCOUVER

Seattle's Volunteer Park Conservatory and Tacoma's W. W. Seymour Botanical Conservatory may look resolutely to the past with their charming Victorian glasshouse construction, but Vancouver's Bloedel Conservatory is a futuristic 70-foot-high dome of plexiglas bubbles covering 15,000 square feet of indoor gardens.

Bloedel Conservatory's innovative air-handling system creates three distinct climates—tropical, desert, and temperate—where over 500 species of plants flourish in naturalistic plantings among ponds, bridges, and a waterfall. The tropical area features palms, orchids, cattleyas, bromeliads, and banana, pineapple, and coffee trees native to Africa, India, Brazil, Java, Mexico, Egypt, Hawaii, and Fiji; the desert area supports collections of cacti and succulents; and the temperate area has seasonal displays of azaleas, rhododendrons, spring bulbs, Easter lilies, summer annuals, and chrysanthemums. Thirty kinds of free-flying tropical birds swoop through the plantings; free bird lists are available for visitors who like to keep count.

W 33rd and Cambie, in Queen Elizabeth Park. Mailing address: Vancouver Board of Parks and Recreation, 2099 Beach Ave, Vancouver, BC V6G IZ4, (604) 872-5513. Apr 15–Sept 30, daily, 10–9; Oct 1–Apr 14, daily, 10–5.
Labels; gift shop; restrooms; wheelchair-accessible; fee.

Richmond Nature Park

RICHMOND

 As their cars speed along the no-man's-land of highways bordering the Richmond Nature Park, it may impress visitors at first glance as one more melancholy example of those truncated and compromised "natural" sites that languish on the fringes of major urban areas. But once they leave their cars behind and slow down to a foot pace, the tranquility and strength of the natural landscape takes over.

Located in the Fraser River estuary, this 100-acre nature park is actually a sphagnum-moss bog where cranberry and blueberry shrubs, salal, hemlock, and other plants native to the region thrive. The park is crisscrossed by several self-guiding trails, none over a mile in length. The pond trail, a boardwalk less than ¼-mile long that features interpretive signs as well as platforms and a tower for viewing birds, makes a good year-round walk for children. The Richmond Nature House at the head of the trail system has exhibits that explain the history and ecology of the park in child-friendly terms.

11851 Westminster Hwy, Richmond, BC V6X 1B4, (604) 273-7015. Daily during daylight hours; phone for open hours at Richmond Nature House. From downtown Vancouver, travel south via Oak Street Bridge, take Richmond Centre exit about 2.4 kilometers (about 1.5 miles) south of the bridge, to Shell Rd; travel south on Shell Rd and turn right onto Westminster Hwy.

Some labels; self-guiding brochures; guided tours; visitors' center; programs; gift shop; picnic facilities; restrooms; wheelchair-accessible; free.

Stanley Park Rose Garden

VANCOUVER

 Set in 1000-acre Stanley Park (which also offers nature trails, stunning wide-angle views of water and mountains, picnic facilities, a zoo, and a first-rate aquarium), the Rose Garden sits on a sunny slope surrounded by handsome perennial borders. Over 3000 rose bushes representing 80 varieties are planted in rather informal beds whose sweeping lines are scaled to the towering conifers that provide the garden's evergreen background. Nearby is a woodsy, vine-covered cottage housing the Stanley Park Zoological Society; its front steps offer a good viewing point for the rose and perennial beds, with romantic Lost Lagoon shimmering on the horizon.

At the west end of Georgia St in downtown Vancouver. (The rose garden is northeast of the main entrance on Pipeline Dr.) Mailing address: Vancouver Board of Parks and Recreation, 2099 Beach Ave, Vancouver, BC V6G 1Z4, (604) 872-5513. Daily during daylight hours.

Restaurants; snack bars; picnic facilities; restrooms; wheelchair-accessible; free.

University of British Columbia Botanical Garden

VANCOUVER

The UBC Botanical Garden resembles a living library of plants from which visitors—browsing through its collections and displays like studious bees—can return home bearing the nectar of horticultural knowledge. The garden feels spacious, partly because there are several planted complexes scattered throughout its 115-acre grounds and partly because it is surrounded by the UBC campus, a 1000-acre enclave of buildings, forest, and shorelines bounded by sweeping views of the Strait of Georgia and the snowy coastal mountain range. With an overall landscape plan developed by a team of botanists, landscape architects, architects, and groundskeepers, the garden's collections and display areas flow gracefully between stands of native woods, presenting visitors with a series of attractive garden rooms in which to flit, dip, and sip at their leisure.

SIGNIFICANT FEATURES

- ◆ collections of Asian plants, Northwest native plants, roses, rhododendrons, and alpines
- ◆ a variety of display gardens, including a winter garden, an arbor garden, a food garden, an evolutionary garden, and a medicinal herb garden

HISTORY

In 1916 the first university-associated botanical garden in Canada was established on a 5-acre site on the UBC campus. By 1966, the botanical garden had grown to 78 acres and featured collections of roses and rhododendrons as well as various perennial beds, with second-growth hemlock and Douglas fir covering the undeveloped acreage.

Four years later, a master plan called for expanding the garden and adding plant collections and display areas that would help carry out a wide-ranging set of institutional objectives. These included the establishment of plant collections for research in the plant sciences, the teaching and training of graduate students, the development of gardener training programs, and plant introduction programs.

In 1982 the Davidson Club was established to help fund the operation and development of the garden; in addition, a group of volunteers, The Friends of the Garden, conduct public tours, operate a seed bank, and assist in developing special garden projects.

THE GARDEN PLAN

Visitors start their tour at the Botanical Garden Office on S.W. Marine Drive, which also is the point of entry to the **David C. Lam Asian Garden,** a collection of plants native to temperate regions in the Far East that have been established under a sheltering canopy of Northwest native firs, hemlocks, and cedars. This exceptionally attractive garden, begun in 1975, features paths winding through 17 acres of species rhododendrons (400 varieties), magnolias, maples, stewartias, perennials, and groundcovers, with vigorous akebias, kiwis, climbing roses, and clematis clambering up the tree trunks and twining around branches 30 feet above the ground. Several boggy streams curl through the garden, making a good growing environment for primulas, ligularias, *Petasites,* and other moisture-loving species. One of the Asian Garden's most spectacular inhabitants is *Cardiocrinum giganteum,* a bulbous herb standing 8 to 10 feet in height whose white lilylike trumpets fling a heady perfume into the air in early summer. (The Asian Garden encompasses 31 acres, of which 14 acres currently remain as native forest, leaving room for future expansion of the collection.)

A wisteria-hung tunnel takes visitors from the Asian Garden to a cluster of plant collections and display gardens on the other side of S.W. Marine Drive, most of which were developed from the 1970 master plan. These areas include the **Food Garden,** with vegetables, berries, grapevines, and espaliered fruit trees especially suitable for regional gardens; the **Arbor Garden,** a handsome wood pergola smothered in wisteria and laburnum; the **Physick Garden,** a circular, brick-paved enclosure featuring medicinal plants; the 8-acre **Native Garden,** featuring 1500 species of plants native to British Columbia, including meadow flowers, grasses, and bog and fen plants; the **E. H. Lohbrunner Alpine Garden,** a 2½-acre west-facing slope strewn with outcroppings of pyroxine andesite, a porous volcanic rock found in central British Columbia, among which are planted alpines and rock plants native to seven geographical areas (Europe, North America, Asia, Asia Minor, Africa, South America, and Australasia); and the **Winter**

Garden, where witch hazels, hellebores, winter-sweets, heathers, viburnums, and daphnes bloom on a sheltered slope opposite the Alpine Garden.

Near the Winter Garden is the intriguing **Evolutionary Garden,** in which ginkgos, ferns, grasses and other primitive plants lining a deep stream give way to deciduous trees and shrubs, which in turn are supplanted by flowering perennials and garden hybrids. The Evolutionary Garden terminates at the Garden Centre, perched atop a gently contoured hill, where new types of groundcovers are being evaluated for introduction to home gardens.

BEST TIMES TO VIEW

The UBC Botanical Garden offers such a wide range of native and exotic plants that a visit at any time of the year is rewarding. In spring magnolias, rhododendrons, primulas, and iris bloom in the Asian Garden, alpines and rock plants flower in the Alpine Garden, and groundcovers splash color over the slopes near the Garden Centre. Perennials, roses, and medicinal herbs in the Physick Garden reach their peak in summer. Fall color is especially attractive in the maples in the Asian Garden.

6804 SW Marine Dr, Vancouver, BC V6T 1Z4, (604) 822-3928. Daily; Mar 16–31, 10–5; Apr 1–May 31, 10–7; June 1–Aug 31, 10–8; Sept 1–30, 10–6; Oct 1–8, 10–5; Oct 9–Mar 15, 10–3. From downtown Vancouver, drive west on W 4th Ave or W 16th Ave to UBC campus and follow signs to Botanical Garden office.

Labels; self-guiding brochures; guided tours available with 2 weeks' notice, (604) 228-4208; classes; workshops; plant sales; horticultural hotline (604) 822-5858; visitors' center; gift shop; restrooms; most of garden wheelchair-accessible; fee (free Oct 9–Mar 15 and every Wed in summer).

NITOBE MEMORIAL GARDEN

The path leading to the gatehouse of Nitobe Memorial Garden winds through magnificent stands of native cedars and firs, which act as atmospheric backdrops for the naturalistic Japanese woodland garden they enclose. In contrast to the formal Japanese gardens in Portland and Seattle, with their ornate hardscapes, complex designs, and exotic plant palettes, Nitobe uses Northwest woodland plants, an uncomplicated, flowing master plan, wood-plank bridges and benches, and a plain stucco teahouse to achieve an atmosphere of rustic tranquility.

The 2½-acre garden was established in 1960 by the University of British

Columbia, the Japanese government, and the local Japanese community to honor the life and accomplishments of Inazo Nitobe (1862–1933), a Japanese philanthropist and advocate of world peace, who died unexpectedly while on a visit to Canada. Nitobe Memorial Garden was designed by Professor Kannosuke Mori, a leader in the contemporary Japanese school of naturalistic landscape architecture, which favors restrained garden plans and elegantly simple hardscapes—an approach which Professor Nitobe, who was a Quaker, surely would have approved of. Japanese gardeners laid out the garden, with Mori personally selecting rocks from nearby Britannia Beach for arrangement in the Tea Garden and for building the waterfall, stream, and pond.

Mori's planting schemes bring out the delicacy inherent in many Northwest native plants. Much of the floor of the south end of the garden is covered in suji moss, which acts as a soft background to the huckleberries, mahonias, salal, and sword and deer ferns composing the understory of this area of the garden. Even in spring, when flowering cherries, marshy beds of iris (13 varieties of *Iris kaempferi* transplanted from a temple garden in Tokyo), and azaleas bloom, Nitobe retains its atmosphere of visual tranquility, making it an outstanding example of a Japanese garden style—the naturalistic woodland garden—seldom seen outside its homeland.

A short path just opposite the entry gate to Nitobe Memorial Garden leads to the **Asian Centre,** a glass and concrete complex with the dramatically plunging roofline of a Japanese country house. The centre is surrounded by a series of stunning side gardens, including a Zen stone and gravel garden, a naturalistic hillside planted in Japanese maples and groundcovers that fronts a formal waterfall, and raised pools that send hypnotic patterns of water rills reflecting against the centre's walls and eaves. Visitors to Nitobe Memorial Garden should be sure to allow themselves enough time to take a stroll through this exceptional landscape.

University of British Columbia campus on NW Marine Dr, just south and across the street from the Museum of Anthropology. March 16–31, daily 10–5; Apr 1–May 31, daily 10–7; June 1–Aug 31, daily 10–8; Sept 1–30, daily 10–6; Oct 1–8, daily 10–5; Oct 9–Mar 15, Mon–Fri 10–3.

Labels; brochures; guided tours Tues and Thurs with 2 weeks' notice, call (604) 731-8982; wheelchair-accessible; fee (free on Wed).

VanDusen Botanical Garden
VANCOUVER

The designers of Vancouver's VanDusen Garden faced an interesting challenge when planning its layout. VanDusen is a botanical garden with a mission to educate the public, so its plant collections had to be arranged according to some botanical system. Yet because the garden places a decided emphasis on horticultural display, those same collections needed to be attractively integrated into a garden setting, a goal that traditional taxonomic grouping—planting separate groves of beeches, magnolias, oaks, and cherries, for instance—seldom achieves.

To solve this problem, the planning staff used the principle of common geographical origin, placing together, for instance, hebes, senecios, and olearias from New Zealand. The staff also decided to overlap and integrate plant collections that are botanically unrelated but share similar growing requirements by planting together, for example, cedars (*Cedrus atlantica* and *C. brevifolia*), rockroses (*Cistus*), and sunroses (*Helianthemum*), all of which prefer poor, dry soils. When the rockroses and sunroses are out of bloom, their foliage continues to create pleasing contrasts in color and texture with the foliage of the cedars. Similarly, collections of hollies and hydrangeas have been interplanted because the twisting, papery branches of the deciduous hydrangeas show off well against the berried hollies in winter, while the hydrangea blooms brighten up the hollies during summer.

Combined with the site's ponds, lakes, waterfall, and massive rockwork, these ingenious plant groupings result in a remarkably beautiful botanical garden, one that easily does double duty as a pleasure garden.

SIGNIFICANT FEATURES
- 39 major plant collections or display gardens on 55 acres of grounds
- a collection of 11 marble garden sculptures, positioned on site by the artists

HISTORY

In 1966 a group of Vancouver citizens advocated turning an abandoned golf course, an unusually attractive site of rolling parkland dotted by stands of Douglas fir and Western red cedar, into a public park. Over the next five years, enthusiasm shifted to developing the site into a botanical garden with parklike vistas. In order to ensure that VanDusen's layout would integrate these two landscape styles smoothly, experts from major European botanical gardens and designers of some of Vancouver's finest public parks were consulted during the planning stages.

In 1971 the golf course was jointly purchased by the city of Vancouver, the private Vancouver Foundation, and the British Columbia provincial government. A massive landscaping program began immediately that reconfigured the site into a flowing, naturalistic landscape of hills, waterfalls, lakes, and streams. The garden was opened to the public in 1975 and is now operated and maintained by the Vancouver Board of Parks and Recreation with the assistance of the advisory board of the Vancouver Botanical Gardens Association.

THE GARDEN PLAN

VanDusen offers visitors plant collections ranging from dwarf conifers to giant redwoods and a group of display areas whose themes run from children's gardens to a formal maze. Some of the major installations include:

- the **Sino-Himalayan Garden,** where a 5-acre site with rock mounds, valleys, pools, and a waterfall shelters Himalayan conifers interplanted with Asian maples, magnolias, and rhododendrons. The Himalayan poppy (*Meconopsis betononicifolia*) can be found blooming here in early summer.

- the **Canadian Heritage Garden,** which is divided into three geographical regions based on the eastern deciduous forest, the western coniferous forest, and the prairie grasslands. In the last of these, a boulder-strewn stream bordered by grasses and wildflowers makes for a particularly enjoyable stroll.

- the **Meditation Garden,** a circle of Douglas firs and camellias entered through a beautiful Japanese-style temple gate.

- a magical woods (near the closed MacMillan Bloedel Place on the garden map) bordering a shallow lake dotted by uprooted snags that look like drowned bonsais.

- the **Mediterranean Garden,** where pungent herbs and subshrubs cascade down rocky slopes capped by several species of true cedars (*Cedrus libani, C. atlantica,* and *C. deodara*).

- collections of bamboo and water lilies spread over a junglelike complex of ponds crossed by floating bridges.

- a glasshouse with displays of Chinese *penjing* and cacti. Nearby is an unusual garden of stone and stonelike (hypertufa) troughs displaying alpines and rock plants from around the world.

Other plant collections include heathers, viburnums, magnolias, Japanese azaleas, camellias, hybrid rhododendrons, roses, and hydrangeas.

Specialty gardens include a formal garden, perennial borders, a Southern Hemisphere garden (with plants from Australia, New Zealand, and South America), and the Stanley Smith Rock Garden.

BEST TIMES TO VIEW

With its wide-ranging collections of plants and display gardens, VanDusen has something to offer every day of the year. (The visitors' pavilion at the entrance features a display of plants currently in bloom or in berry, along with maps and self-guiding brochures to help locate them.) In spring camellias, magnolias, rhododendrons, azaleas, cherries, crabapples, and viburnums flower; summer brings on the rose garden, perennial beds, water lilies, and hydrangeas. In fall many of the tree collections, notably the Japanese maples, ginkgos, and sweet gums, display their foliage at their peak of color. In winter the conifer and bamboo collections appear at their most dramatic under light coverings of snow, while hollies, witch hazels, and heathers add bright blooms or berries.

5251 Oak St, Vancouver, BC V6M 4H1, (604) 266-7194. Daily, June–Aug 10–9, Sept 10–6, Oct–Mar 10–4, Apr 10–6, May 10–8. Closed Christmas Day. From Hwy 99, turn east to Oak St just north of Oak St Bridge; the garden is on the corner of Oak and 37th Ave.

Labels; brochures; guided tours Sundays at 2 (at 3 in summer); visitors' center; programs; classes; plant sales; gift shop; restaurant; restrooms; wheel-chair-accessible; fee.

Sendall Gardens

LANGLEY

Visiting this spot for the first time is exhilarating, rather like jumping a wall to explore someone's secret garden. It's filled with the kinds of delightful touches—peacock pens, rose arbors, an open-roofed gazebo through which sprays of flowering cherries hang—that only an imaginative gardener who is in love with his or her site can devise.

The 4-acre property had been a private home and garden for several generations before the Langley Parks and Recreation Department acquired it in the mid-1970s. At that time it featured a small duck pond and some fine old rhododendrons, Japanese maples, and cedars, but much of the ground was smothered by alder, salmonberry, and other Northwest forest "weeds." From 1975 to 1985, parks department foreman Bill Heubener, who lived in a caretaker's cottage on site, undertook what he calls "a labor of love" in transforming the grounds into today's multi-roomed garden.

The front garden, now open and sunny, originally was a flat, featureless tract with few significant plants. Heubener bermed the area with soil excavated from other city projects and established thick plantings of flowering cherries, rhododendrons, and other ornamental shrubs. To give it an attractive framework, he established wide paths, rustic trellises covered in grapevines, and a small fountain and pool.

Behind the caretaker's cottage, a wide, woodsy ravine features paths winding around two ponds. Heubener maintained the natural look of this woodland area while adding Chinese dogwoods, oaks, larches, and redbuds for variation in leaf texture and color. Of particular note here is the "Wisteria Jungle," a tangle of *Wisteria floribunda* that twines over bigleaf maples and cedars to a height of 40 feet.

Next to the cottage is a small greenhouse, where such exotics as figs, palms, plumeria, and philodendrons flourish among seasonal blooming plants. Nearby are some stands of mature rhododendrons, trellises covered in clematis and climbing hydrangeas, and pens for peacocks and waterfowl.

Corner of 201 A St and 50th Ave; no phone. Info: City of Langley, 5549 204th St, Langley, BC V3A 1Z4, (604) 530-3131. Daily during daylight hours. From Vancouver, take Hwy 1A (Fraser Hwy) about 40 kilometers (about 25 miles) east to Langley, turn right (south) at 200th St, and then left (east) at 50th Ave.
Picnic tables; restrooms; limited wheelchair access; free.

Minter Gardens
ROSEDALE

Minter Gardens is an amalgamation of formal and informal garden rooms clustered on 15 acres of forested slopes, glens, and ponds in mountain foothills 120 kilometers (75 miles) east of Vancouver. Owners Brian and Faye Minter, who opened the gardens to the public in 1980, have given each area a distinct theme and atmosphere, with natural woods sometimes used as buffer zones between them.

Some of these areas display a pleasantly informal style that makes sensitive use of the topography. These include the **Rhododendron Garden,** with its flowering shrubs on a shady slope bordered by ponds and a stream, and the **Hillside Garden,** where a mixture of dwarf conifers, ferns, groundcovers, and hybrid annuals and perennials are planted among rocky outcrops.

Other areas are more formal, such as the **Rose Garden,** with its Victorian gazebo set in the middle of concentric rose beds, and the **Formal Garden,** where a central rectangle of turf is bordered by planting beds surrounded by clipped box-wood hedges. Of special note is a rock *penjing* collection in the Chinese pavilion, reputed to be the largest such collection outside the People's Republic of China. Minter Gardens also features a hanging-basket arbor, a maze, aviaries, a duck pond, peacock pens, and a play area for children.

52892 Bunker Rd, Rosedale, BC V2P 1X0, (604) 794-7191. Mailing address: P.O. Box 40, Chilliwack, BC V2P 6H7. Apr 1–Oct 30, daily 9–dusk. From Vancouver, take Trans-Canada Hwy 1 about 120 kilometers (about 75 miles) east to Harrison Hot Springs exit and follow signs.

Brochure; gift shop; restaurant; snack bar; picnic tables; restrooms; wheelchair-accessible; fee.

Butchart Gardens, *Victoria*

Vancouver Island
Beacon Hill Park
VICTORIA

This 150-acre park, established in the 1850s on land set aside by the Hudson's Bay Company, features a century-old cricket pitch, picturesque stone bridges, a rose garden, towering canopies of mature firs, cedars, and oaks, and ornamental shrubs. Gardeners may find the following displays of special interest: sumptuous perennial borders near the cricket pitch, south of Queen's Lake; rocky outcroppings in a naturalistic setting at the north end of the park, where naturalized daffodils spread in golden pools in spring; and crescent-shaped perennial and annual beds north of the putting green, which pack a special wallop in high to late summer.

VANCOUVER ISLAND, BRITISH COLUMBIA

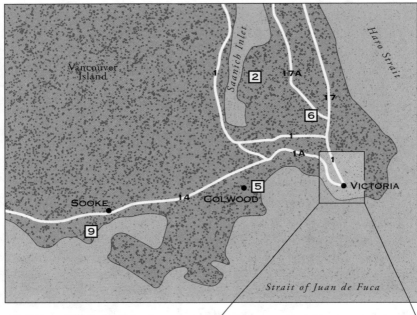

1. Beacon Hill Park, *Victoria*
2. Butchart Gardens, *Victoria*
3. Crystal Garden, *Victoria*
4. Government House Gardens, *Victoria*
5. Hatley Castle, *Colwood*
6. Horticulture Centre of the Pacific, *Victoria*
7. Native Plant Garden at the Royal British Columbia Museum, *Victoria*
8. Point Ellice House, *Victoria*
9. Sooke Harbour House Gardens, *Sooke*

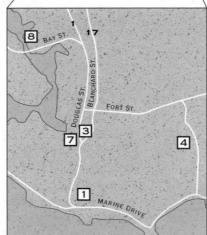

Corner of Douglas and Superior sts in downtown Victoria, (604) 361-0613.
Daily during daylight hours.
   Restrooms; some wheelchair access; free.

Butchart Gardens

VICTORIA

 With a quarter of a million visitors entering its vine-wreathed portals every year, Butchart Gardens ranks as one of Canada's most popular outdoor attractions west of Niagara Falls. Like Niagara, Butchart Gardens puts on quite a show—from thousands of bright annuals cascading down a sunken garden's rocky walls to colored lights rippling over fountains jetting 50 feet into the night sky.

SIGNIFICANT FEATURES

- ◆ 55 acres of impeccably maintained floral displays
- ◆ an Italian Garden, a Rose Garden, and a Sunken Garden

HISTORY

The gardens started in 1904 as the private estate of Robert Butchart, a successful producer of Portland cement. Over a period of 40 years, Butchart and his wife, Jenny, developed several distinct garden rooms on the original site, populating them with plants brought back from their travels around the world. Still owned and managed by members of the Butchart family, the gardens have been open to the public for over 50 years.

THE GARDEN PLAN

In the early stages of developing the estate gardens, the Butcharts took on a major challenge to transform an immense, mined-out limestone quarry with 50-foot-high walls of bare rock into the **Sunken Garden.** They covered the desolate walls with sprays of ivy and cotoneaster, constructed a waterfall and a pond, and planted a permanent backdrop of trees and flowering shrubs, including rhododendrons, pieris, hydrangeas, and azaleas. Today mounds of annuals in hot corals, scarlets, golds, and purples pulse along the quarry floor in summer, their reflections blooming like exotic algae in the central pond's still waters.

   The path from the Sunken Garden winds up to a viewing point that overlooks yet another massive pond, this one surrounded by conifers and other Pacific Northwest trees and shrubs. Ross Fountain erupts from its center in jets that create patterns of water and light against the sky. Visitors leave this tranquil spot to encounter Butchart Garden's three most formal garden rooms.

The **Rose Garden** features rustic wood trellises smothered in old-fashioned climbers and informal planting beds where shrub roses are thickly interplanted with complementary perennials, including delphiniums, asters, and nicotianas. It's an exceptionally attractive site that manages to avoid the gawky, stiff layout that often characterizes more formal rose gardens.

Nearby is the **Japanese Garden,** whose uninspired plantings and nondescript hardscapes call out for renovation. The **Italian Garden,** which brings visitors full circle on their garden tour, is a classical confection of raised pools, ivied colonnades, and geometric planting beds that provides a refreshing spot in which to linger during the heat of the day.

During the summer months the gardens are lighted for night viewing; fireworks programs are offered every Saturday night during July and August.

BEST TIMES TO VIEW

Butchart Gardens maintains consistent displays of blooms from May through September, but special times to visit include mid-spring, when 300,000 bulbs are in full regalia, and mid- to late summer, when the Rose Garden hits its stride.

Benvenuto Road. Mailing address: P.O. Box 4010, Station A, Victoria, BC V8X 3X4, (604) 652-4422. Daily, May–June 9–9, July–Aug 9–11, Sept 9–9, Oct–Nov 9–4, Dec (when there is a special Christmas light display) 9–8, Jan–Feb 9–4, Mar–Apr 9–5. From Victoria, travel approximately 16 kilometers (10 miles) north on Hwy 17 to Butchart-Brentwood exit; turn left at Keating Rd and then continue another 8.8 kilometers (5.5 miles).

Brochures; gift shop; restaurants; picnic tables; restrooms; wheelchair-accessible; fee.

Crystal Garden
VICTORIA

 Built in 1925 by Canadian Pacific Railroad, the original Crystal Garden was a block-long conservatory with tearooms, ballrooms, and an immense saltwater swimming pool. For close to 50 years the garden served as a hub of Victoria's social and athletic events, until prohibitive maintenance costs forced its closure in 1971.

Recognizing the Crystal Garden's historical significance, the Province of British Columbia bought and thoroughly renovated the building; today a provincial agency administers the garden, which exhibits plants, rare birds, and small mammals from tropical and subtropical areas of the world. The garden display fills most of the first floor. The mezzanine supports a restaurant where afternoon tea is served—it's a less grand affair than the tea offered at the Empress Hotel across the street, but the surroundings are pleasantly lush. (And how often is one able to drink tea to the shrieks of the cockatoo and laughing kookaburra?)

About 150 species of plants, most of them labeled, are displayed in the main garden area; collections include palms, calatheas, bromeliads, daturas, and orchids. Other exhibits include ornate aviaries containing 70 species of tropical and subtropical birds, and a series of glassed-in cases that display golden tamarinds and pygmy marmosets.

The plant and animal displays are meant to entertain rather than to reproduce specific ecosystems, so visitors will encounter some charmingly scrambled tableaux: tropical orchids massed near the replica of an Italian stone fountain filled with Japanese koi, and carved New Guinea statues looming over an exhibit of black-footed penguins native to an island off South Africa. On a recent evening visit, flamingos preened and fluttered while a dance band in the garden's ballroom ran through a dizzying repertoire of cowboy swing, sambas, polkas, and mariachi music. Altogether, this is an endearing spot to while away an evening or a rainy day.

700 block of Douglas St, directly behind the Empress Hotel in downtown Victoria, (604) 381-1213. Daily, July–Aug 9–9, Sept–June 10–5:30.
    Labels; brochures; restaurant/tearoom; restrooms; wheelchair-accessible; fee.

Government House Gardens
VICTORIA

 Government House has served as the official residence of British Columbia's Lieutenant Governor since the days when Canada was a colony, and some of the garden areas dotted around its 35 acres have been in existence for over 100 years. Many of the Lieutenant Governors and their spouses improved and expanded the grounds during their time in office, resulting in a series of gracious garden rooms that display a variety of landscape styles and plant palettes. Most reflect a decidedly English taste and approach, making this the proper garden to stroll in after a sumptuous afternoon tea.

SIGNIFICANT FEATURES

- 10 acres of public gardens, including sweeping lawns with stands of firs and evergreen shrubs, a naturalistic pond, dramatic rocky outcrops, and a Victorian rose garden framed by wrought-iron pergolas
- unusually lovely perennial borders in the E. Jane Rogers garden

HISTORY

Several houses have stood on the present-day grounds, the original one having been built in the 1850s as the private residence of Vancouver Island's first Attorney General. That house was expanded and renovated while it served as the Colonial Governor's residence during the next half century; in 1899 it burned to the ground, and a new mansion was built on the same spot. When this residence also burned in 1957, the present house was built.

In the 1800s the grounds featured Pacific Northwest shrubs and trees; native oaks (*Garrya* sp.) 200 to 500 years old remain today as mementos of the original landscape. In the early 1900s ornamental trees, shrubs, and lawns were introduced; many of them, carefully pruned and rejuvenated, still dot the present grounds.

The gardens waxed and waned under succeeding administrations, and by the 1960s sizable areas in front of the house were overgrown. Fortunately, Major-General George Pearkes, a keen gardener, became Lieutenant Governor at this time, and he embarked on a personal mission to reclaim the gardens. Donning his leather gaiters and trusty wellies, Pearkes would attack the decrepit beds and borders with zeal practically every morning. One day an out-of-province visitor observed him digging a bed and, bursting with indignant pity, told him she meant to scold the groundskeepers for working an old man so hard. Apparently His Honor threw down his trowel and said, "Madam, I wish to heaven you would!"

Today, archivists are researching old photographs and documents pertaining to the grounds and over 100 volunteers are assisting the garden staff in renovating the gardens.

THE GARDEN PLAN

A country garden featuring informal mixes of perennials and annuals lies to the right of the main entry gates. To the left stands an old rhododendron grove, beyond which lies a naturalistic pond fringed with grasses and bamboos. Moving away from the pond toward the house, visitors see rock outcroppings almost smothered in roses, hydrangeas, ferns, and mosses. Off the west side of the house, a deep slope features phalanxes of bulbs in spring and annuals all through the summer.

Visitors may feel moved to offer a special gardener's prayer of thanks to Mrs. E. Jane Rogers, a former Government House resident who, as recently as 1988, added extensive new perennial borders of great beauty and sophistication to the grounds. Immediately adjacent to the country garden near the main entrance, the Rogers garden features a white and silver border where heaps of white cosmos, *Nicotiana sylvestris,* woolly lamb's ears, and creamy phlox shimmer in the late summer sun, with complementary touches of color contributed by spiky metal-blue cardoons and pink climbing roses edged with silver. The opposite border ripples from lavender to gold to orange, and features peach-sherbet poppies glowing against a purple smoke tree (*Cotinus coggygria* 'Purpurea')—a dramatic combination of colors and textures. The pergola behind these borders leads to a sunken Edwardian rose garden, where stone griffins brood over hybrid and old-fashioned shrub roses.

The present Lieutenant Governor, David C. Lam, is a devoted gardener who contributed to the development of the Dr. Sun Yat-Sen Classical Chinese Garden in Vancouver as well as to the collection of Asian plants at the University of British Columbia. He is also assisting in the development of a new Victorian rose garden at Government House, based on the design of the rose garden that once flourished at Warwick Castle in England; it features old-fashioned single roses in shades of pink and white.

A 22-acre woodland native plant garden west of the residence opens to the public in 1993.

BEST TIMES TO VIEW

The grounds are at their best from mid-April through early September; there is quite a bit of winter bloom throughout the cold season as well.

1401 Rockland Ave, Victoria, BC V8S 1V9, (604) 387-2080. Daily during daylight hours. From Inner Harbour in downtown Victoria, take Fort St east to Cook St, turn right and travel to Rockland Ave, then turn left onto Rockland. No restrooms; some wheelchair access; free.

Hatley Castle
COLWOOD

Established in 1908 as the estate of a regional tycoon and serving since 1940 as the campus of Royal Roads Military College, the grounds at Hatley Castle feature formal and informal gardens surrounded by a sweeping naturalistic landscape. Although the grounds continue to be kept in the grand, turn-of-the-century style in which they were originally planted, subtle martial touches have appeared over the past several decades—from tidy rows of flowers ranked in color-coordinated blocks, to stone statues of Neptune sternly prodding dolphins with a dripping trident, to uniformed cadets who dodge the peacocks that strut through the gardens with a tight military precision.

SIGNIFICANT FEATURES
- 650 acres that include a formal Italian garden, a naturalistic Japanese garden, and a lush waterside garden
- classical stone pergolas, terraces, and balustrades

HISTORY
James Dunsmuir was a Victoria railroad and coal magnate who built Hatley Castle during his tenure as British Columbia's Lieutenant Governor between 1906 and 1909. It's a rather overwhelming stone pile with Gothic overtones, featuring ivy-covered turrets and classical balustrades that command views of Esquimalt Lagoon. Dunsmuir tacked an Italian garden with graceful classical hardscapes onto one wing of the castle, established impressive perennial borders and squares of lawn stretching out toward the lagoon, and bordered these formal gardens with naturalistic plantings. Inside the castle, Dunsmuir constructed an ornate conservatory housing tropical plants native to the Empire's more exotic colonial outposts.

Dunsmuir died in 1920, and his widow lived on in Hatley Castle until her death in 1937. The Canadian government then bought the estate and established a military training college there three years later. Today the castle itself is open to the public only on special occasions, but the grounds can be visited daily year-round.

THE GARDEN PLAN
Visitors enter the gardens by a long flight of stone steps punctuated by urns bristling with blue palms and statues of prowling lions. From a small forecourt near the entry to the castle, visitors walk around to the grand terrace at

the back, where they encounter the three most formal areas of the grounds. The **Italian Garden** is an altogether charming outdoor room with stone pergolas and colonnades that are draped in wisteria and clematis in late spring and early summer. Planting beds are hedged by clipped boxwoods and filled in mid- to late summer with orderly rows of dahlias, celosias, and marigolds in the boldest shades of scarlet and gold. Stone stairs descend to the **Sunken Garden,** where opposing borders of "cool" and "warm" perennials fringe a formal lawn. Formal parterres outlined in boxwood and filled with lavender edge a somber but elegant water-lily pool.

Visitors leave the formal areas through wrought-iron gates and follow a gravel path edged by a stream that leads to the more naturalistic garden areas. The pleasantly informal, lushly overgrown 4-acre **Japanese Garden** features gently hilly terrain and a large central pond with several water pavilions whose ornate wood balconies are reflected on the water's still surface. Below the Japanese garden is a quite enchanting waterside garden on the banks of Esquimalt Lagoon. Reached by walking along a series of gently gushing waterchutes, this area supports stands of bamboo interplanted with gunnera, ligularia, hostas, primulas, and other plants with lush growth habits and watery associations.

As visitors retrace their steps from the lagoon through the Japanese Garden, they encounter a stucco wall with a deep fringe of camellias, hydrangeas, and lilies that leads to an oval rose garden backed by perennial borders and a tennis court. A path abutting classrooms and dormitories leads back to the castle.

BEST TIMES TO VIEW

Wisteria, camellias, flowering cherries, and rhododendrons bloom in spring. Summer brings on the annual and perennial beds and summer-flowering shrubs such as hydrangeas and climbing roses. Japanese maples, asters, and chrysanthemums offer fine autumn color.

Mailing address: F.M.O. Victoria, BC VOS 1BO, (604) 388-1660. Daily, 10-4. From Victoria, travel about 10 kilometers (about 6.2 miles) east on Hwy 1-1A toward the suburb of Colwood; approximately 0.1 kilometer (0.6 mile) past turn-off sign for Fort Rodd Hill Rd, look on left side of highway for entrance to Royal Roads Military College.

Campus restrooms; limited wheelchair access; free.

Horticulture Centre of the Pacific
VICTORIA

 The grounds here serve as a kind of open-air laboratory, where volunteers from Vancouver Island garden clubs cooperatively experiment with organic gardening techniques on a variety of plants especially suited to local growing conditions. The centre's pleasantly rural 6-acre campus features well-labeled displays of annuals, perennials, hybrid and old roses, herbs, flowering shrubs, winter-blooming plants, and rock plants. An arboretum is currently being established.

Visitors are welcome to bring a picnic and wander through the grounds. After browsing the flower and herb displays on a hot summer day, it's refreshing to pull up a wooden garden chair on the centre's circular gravel court to view the cool green valley spread out below.

505 Quayle Rd, Victoria, BC V8X 3X1, (604) 479-6162. Daily during daylight hours. From Victoria, take Hwy 17 to Royal Oak exit and travel west on Royal Oak Dr; turn right on W Saanich Rd, left onto Beaver Lake Rd, and left onto Elk Rd; continue to Quayle Rd. The centre is about 7 kilometers (4.4 miles) north of Victoria.

Labels; brochures; tours; visitors' center; programs; classes; plant sales; picnic facilities; restrooms; wheelchair-accessible; fee.

Native Plant Garden
at the Royal British Columbia Museum
VICTORIA

Dotted about the Royal British Columbia Museum's grounds are seven mini-environments—a Sand Dune Bed, a Dry Interior Garden, an Alpine Garden, a Wetland Garden, an Oregon Grape Bed, a Camas Bed, and a Coast Forest Garden—which display 300 species of plants native to British Columbia growing in their appropriate natural settings.

The grounds of the Parliament Buildings, directly across Government Street from the museum, feature some pleasant fountains and beds of annuals set among acres of rolling green lawn.

Government and Belleville sts in downtown Victoria, (604) 387-2423. Daily during daylight hours.

Labels; self-guiding brochures available in museum lobby; guided tours May–Sept; restrooms; wheelchair-accessible; free.

Point Ellice House
VICTORIA

Roses curling around painted wooden shutters, clematis scrambling up trellises, spacious lawns sloping down to open water, and neat white picket fences hedging trees and flower beds—these features help create the unpretentious, thoroughly appealing charm that clings to this restored Victorian house and garden.

Built in 1867 by Peter O'Reilly, a district magistrate, Point Ellice House served as the residence of his family and their descendants until 1975, when the provincial government acquired the property and began a historically accurate renovation of the 1½-acre site. Diaries, garden catalogs, and bills of sale found in the attic are being used to reconstruct the garden as it existed between 1889 and 1914, from the crushed-gravel driveway sweeping the front of the house to the tiny orchard bordering the back garden.

The reconstruction is especially noteworthy as one of the few in our region that brings back to life a turn-of-the-century middle-class home and garden. Estates such as Victoria's Hatley Castle and Washington State's Lakewold and Bloedel Reserve were built on a grand scale by the region's aristocracy; in contrast, Point Ellice House recreates the charming atmosphere achieved in the homes and gardens of Victoria's comfortable professional class during an era of easily acquired land and comparative domestic leisure.

The O'Reillys established rhododendrons and hollies among the native firs and madrones in their front garden, while in the back they created a croquet lawn flanked by a small rose garden and a kitchen garden. Around the house stone-lined planting beds feature hydrangeas, hardy fuchsias (*F. magellanica*), lilacs, hostas, honeysuckle, roses, and a froth of annuals and perennials. (The 9-foot hollyhocks in these beds descend from seeds originally planted there by O'Reillys several generations ago.) The design of these areas seems natural and unforced, and their appeal is correspondingly straightforward.

Strolling the grounds of Point Ellice House makes one nostalgic for a past in which gardens—fussed over, cherished, and lived in—were centers of family activity. Such nostalgia is made the more poignant by the sound of trucks roaring and rattling their way to a modern industrial area farther down the street. How tempting to stay a little longer within the enchanted bounds of the white picket fence, dreaming of croquet games played on a hot summer afternoon, and of tea served on the lawn underneath the shade trees by the water's edge.

2616 Pleasant St; no phone. Info: Heritage Properties Branch, Ministry of Tourism and Culture, 800 Johnson St, Victoria, BC V6V 1X4, (604) 387-4697. Mid–June through early Sept, Thurs–Mon 11–5; rest of Sept, Suns only 11–5. From downtown Victoria, travel west on Bay St; just before Bay St Bridge, turn north (right) on Pleasant St.

Brochures; sometimes tea is served on the lawn in July and August (call for dates); restrooms; limited wheelchair access; fee.

Sooke Harbour House Gardens
SOOKE

Surrounding a two-story country inn noted for its accommodations and fine dining, several large berms display fruit trees, vegetables, herbs, and edible flowers in an attractively informal jumble. A hillside overlooking the beach features mounds of nasturtiums, sea thistles, yarrows, onions, daisies, lavenders, and native blackberries that seem to tumble down into Sooke Harbour below. Reservations are required for dining, but non-dining visitors may wander through this compact garden during daylight hours.

1528 Whiffen Spit Rd, R. R. 4, Sooke, BC V0S 1N0, (604) 642-3421. From Victoria, follow Hwy 1 for 37 kilometers (23 miles) west to Sooke/Colwood turnoff (Hwy 14); follow Hwy 14 1.6 kilometers (1 mile) past Sooke and turn left on Whiffen Spit Road.

No restrooms; some wheelchair access; free.

Gardens by Type

 Arboreta and Gardens with Notable Tree Collections
  Bloedel Reserve—Bainbridge Island, Washington
* Carl S. English, Jr., Botanical Gardens—Seattle, Washington
* Elk Rock, the Garden of the Bishop's Close—Portland, Oregon
* Hoyt Arboretum—Portland, Oregon
* John A. Finch Arboretum—Spokane, Washington
  Lakewold—Tacoma, Washington
* Mount Pisgah Arboretum—Eugene, Oregon
* Point Defiance Park—Tacoma, Washington
* Sehome Hill Arboretum—Bellingham, Washington
* Washington Park Arboretum—Seattle, Washington
  University of British Columbia Botanical Garden—Vancouver, British Columbia
  VanDusen Botanical Garden—Vancouver, British Columbia

 Asian Gardens
  Asian Garden, University of British Columbia Botanical Garden—
  Vancouver, British Columbia
  Bloedel Reserve—Bainbridge Island, Washington
  Dr. Sun Yat-Sen Classical Chinese Garden—Vancouver, British Columbia
* Eastern Garden, Bellevue Botanical Garden— Bellevue, Washington
* Japanese Friendship Garden—New Westminster, British Columbia
* Japanese Garden, Hatley Castle—Victoria, British Columbia
* Japanese Garden, Point Defiance Park—Tacoma, Washington
  Japanese Garden, Washington Park Arboretum—Seattle, Washington
* Kubota Gardens—Seattle, Washington
  Nitobe Memorial Garden, University of British Columbia Botanical Garden—
  Vancouver, British Columbia

(*) denotes free admission.

* Pacific Rim Bonsai Collection—Federal Way, Washington
* Penjing Collection at the International Buddhist Society Temple—Richmond, British Columbia
  Penjing Collection, Minter Gardens—Rosedale, British Columbia
  Penjing Collection, VanDusen Botanical Garden—Vancouver, British Columbia
  Portland Japanese Garden—Portland, Oregon
* Shore Acres State Park Botanical Garden—Coos Bay, Oregon
* Spokane Nishinomiya Japanese Garden, Manito Park and Botanical Gardens— Spokane, Washington
  Yashiro Japanese Garden—Olympia, Washington

 ## Botanical Gardens

* Bellevue Botanical Garden—Bellevue, Washington
* Berry Botanic Garden—Portland, Oregon
* Carl S. English, Jr., Botanical Gardens—Seattle, Washington
* Leach Botanical Garden—Portland, Oregon
* Manito Park and Botanical Gardens—Spokane, Washington
* Medicinal Herb Garden—Seattle, Washington
* Shore Acres State Park Botanical Garden—Coos Bay, Oregon
  University of British Columbia Botanical Garden—Vancouver, British Columbia
  VanDusen Botanical Garden—Vancouver, British Columbia

 ## Conservatories

  Bloedel Conservatory, Queen Elizabeth Park—Vancouver, British Columbia
  Crystal Garden—Victoria, British Columbia
* Gaiser Conservatory, Manito Park and Botanical Gardens—Spokane, Washington
* Volunteer Park Conservatory—Seattle, Washington
* W. W. Seymour Botanical Conservatory—Tacoma, Washington
* Washington State Capitol Grounds Conservatory—Olympia, Washington

 ## Display, Demonstration, and Estate Gardens— Displays of Trees, Shrubs, and/or Perennials

* Beacon Hill Park Perennial Borders—Victoria, British Columbia
* Bellevue Downtown Park—Bellevue, Washington
  Bloedel Reserve—Bainbridge Island, Washington
  Butchart Gardens—Victoria, British Columbia
* Carnation Research Farm Gardens—Carnation, Washington
* Chetzemokah Park—Port Townsend, Washington

* Children's Hospital and Medical Center Perennial Borders—Seattle, Washington
* Deepwood Gardens—Salem, Oregon
* Elk Rock, the Garden of the Bishop's Close—Portland, Oregon
  Fantasy Garden World—Richmond, British Columbia
  Froggwell Garden—Freeland, Washington
* Government House Gardens—Victoria, British Columbia
* Hatley Castle—Colwood, British Columbia
  Horticulture Centre of the Pacific—Victoria, British Columbia
* Hovander Homestead/Tennant Lake Nature Walk/Fragrance Garden—Ferndale,
    Washington
* Hulda Klager Lilac Gardens—Woodland, Washington
* Jenkins Estate—Aloha, Oregon
  La Conner Flats Display Garden—La Conner, Washington
  Lakewold—Tacoma, Washington
* Lewis and Clark College Campus—Portland, Oregon
* Manito Park and Botanical Gardens—Spokane, Washington
* Medicinal Herb Garden—Seattle, Washington
  Minter Gardens—Rosedale, British Columbia
  Ohme Gardens—Wenatchee, Washington
* Orcas Hotel Garden—Orcas Island, Washington
* Park & Tilford Gardens—North Vancouver, British Columbia
* Pioneer Garden at Fort Vancouver National Historic Site—Vancouver,
    Washington
* Parsons Gardens—Seattle, Washington
* Point Defiance Park—Tacoma, Washington
  Point Ellice House—Victoria, British Columbia
* Puget Gardens—Tacoma, Washington
* Queen Elizabeth Park—Vancouver, British Columbia
  Rhododendron Species Foundation Display Gardens—Federal Way, Washington
* Roche Harbor Garden—San Juan Island, Washington
* Sendall Gardens—Langley, British Columbia
* Shore Acres State Park Botanical Garden—Coos Bay, Oregon
* Sooke Harbour House Gardens—Sooke, British Columbia
* Tilth and Good Shepherd Demonstration Gardens—Seattle, Washington
  VanDusen Botanical Garden—Vancouver, British Columbia

Native Plant Collections
    * Bellevue Botanical Garden—Bellevue, Washington
* Berry Botanic Garden—Portland Oregon

Bloedel Reserve—Bainbridge Island, Washington
* Carl S. English, Jr., Botanical Gardens—Seattle, Washington
* Darlingtonia Botanical Wayside—Florence, Oregon
* Erna Gunther Ethnobotanical Garden—Seattle, Washington
* Goodfellow Grove, Center for Urban Horticulture—Seattle, Washington
* Hoyt Arboretum—Portland Oregon
* John A. Finch Arboretum—Spokane, Washington
* John Inskeep Environmental Learning Center—Oregon City, Oregon
* Leach Botanical Garden—Portland, Oregon
* Mount Pisgah Arboretum—Eugene, Oregon
* Native Arboretum, Queen Elizabeth Park—Vancouver, British Columbia
* Native Plant Area, Park & Tilford Gardens—North Vancouver, British Columbia
* Native Plant Garden, Point Defiance Park—Tacoma, Washington
* Native Plant Garden at the Royal British Columbia Museum—Victoria, British
    Columbia
  Native Plant Garden, University of British Columbia Botanical Garden—
    Vancouver, British Columbia
*Native Woodland Garden, Government House—Victoria, British Columbia
*Sehome Hill Arboretum—Bellingham, Washington
*Washington Park Arboretum—Seattle, Washington

Natural Areas
                * Darlingtonia Botanical Wayside—Florence, Oregon
* Foster Island—Washington Park Arboretum, Seattle, Washington
* Kah Tai Lagoon Nature Park—Port Townsend, Washington
* Mount Pisgah Arboretum—Eugene, Oregon
* Point Defiance Park—Tacoma, Washington
* Rhododendron Park—Coupeville, Washington
* Richmond Nature Park—Richmond, British Columbia
* Sehome Hill Arboretum—Bellingham, Washington
* South Slough Estuarine Reserve—Charleston, Oregon
* Tennant Lake Nature Walk—Ferndale, Washington

Rhododendron Gardens
        Cecil and Molly Smith Rhododendron Garden—St. Paul, Oregon
* Crystal Springs Rhododendron Garden—Portland, Oregon
* Hendricks Park Rhododendron Garden—Eugene, Oregon
  Meerkerk Rhododendron Gardens—Greenbank, Washington
  Rhododendron Species Foundation Display Gardens—Federal Way, Washington

Rhododendron collections are also found in other regional gardens, notably the Asian Garden at the University of British Columbia Botanical Garden; Bellevue Botanical Garden; Berry Botanic Garden; Bloedel Reserve; Elk Rock, the Garden of the Bishop's Close; La Conner Flats Display Garden; Lakewold; VanDusen Botanical Garden; and Washington Park Arboretum.

Rose Gardens

* Bush's Pasture Park—Salem, Oregon
  Butchart Gardens—Victoria, British Columbia
* Fairhaven Rose Garden—Bellingham, Washington
  Fantasy Garden World—Richmond, British Columbia
* George Owen Memorial Rose Garden—Eugene, Oregon
* Government House Gardens—Victoria, British Columbia
* International Rose Test Garden—Portland, Oregon
* Jackson & Perkins Test and Display Garden—Medford, Oregon
  Minter Gardens—Rosedale, British Columbia
* Park & Tilford Gardens—North Vancouver, British Columbia
* Point Defiance Park—Tacoma, Washington
* Queen Elizabeth Park—Vancouver, British Columbia
* Rose Hill, Manito Park and Botanical Gardens—Spokane, Washington
* Rothschild House—Port Townsend, Washington
* Stanley Park Rose Garden—Vancouver, British Columbia
* The Sunken Rose Garden—Portland, Oregon
  Tallina's Garden—Clackamas, Oregon
  VanDusen Botanical Garden—Vancouver, British Columbia
* Woodland Park Rose Garden—Seattle, Washington

OTHER GARDEN CATEGORIES

Child-Friendly Gardens

  Butchart Gardens—Victoria, British Columbia
* Carnation Research Farm Gardens—Carnation, Washington
  Crystal Garden—Victoria, British Columbia
  Fantasy Garden World—Ricmond, British Columbia
  Minter Gardens—Rosedale, British Columbia
* Point Defiance Park—Tacoma, Washington
* Richmond Nature Park—Richmond, British Columbia
* Sendall Gardens—Langley, British Columbia
* Tennant Lake Nature Walk/Fragrance Garden/Hovander Homestead—Ferndale, Washington

VanDusen Botanical Garden—Vancouver, British Columbia
* Volunteer Park Conservatory—Seattle, Washington
Walker Rock Garden—Seattle, Washington
Washington Park Zoo Grounds—Portland, Oregon
Woodland Park Zoological Gardens—Seattle, Washington

Gardens Available for Private Functions
Crystal Garden—Victoria, British Columbia
Deepwood Gardens—Salem, Oregon
Dr. Sun Yat-Sen Classical Chinese Garden—Vancouver, British Columbia
Jenkins Estate—Aloha, Oregon
La Conner Flats Display Garden—La Conner, Washington
Lakewold—Tacoma, Washington
Park & Tilford Gardens—North Vancouver, British Columbia
Parsons Gardens—Seattle, Washington
Point Defiance Park Japanese Garden Pavilion—Tacoma, Washington
Point Ellice House—Victoria, British Columbia

Gardens for Picnicking
* Chetzemokah Park—Port Townsend, Washington
* Darlingtonia Botanical Wayside—Florence, Oregon
* Hendricks Park Rhododendron Garden—Eugene, Oregon
Horticulture Centre of the Pacific—Victoria, British Columbia
* Hoyt Arboretum—Portland, Oregon
* International Rose Test Garden—Portland, Oregon
* Manito Park and Botanical Garden—Spokane, Washington
Minter Gardens—Rosedale, British Columbia
* Point Defiance Park—Tacoma, Washington
* Puget Gardens—Tacoma, Washington
* Queen Elizabeth Park—Vancouver, British Columbia
* Rhododendron Park—Coupeville, Washington
* Shore Acres State Park Botanical Gardens—Coos Bay, Oregon
* Hovander Homestead—Ferndale, Washington

Gardens of Winter Interest
* Berry Botanic Garden—Portland, Oregon
Bloedel Reserve—Bainbridge Island, Washington
* Elk Rock, Garden of the Bishop's Close—Portland, Oregon
* Joseph A. Witt Winter Garden, Washington Park Arboretum—Seattle, Washington

* Leach Botanical Garden—Portland, Oregon
* Parsons Gardens—Seattle, Washington
  Winter Garden, Horticulture Centre of the Pacific—Victoria, British Columbia
  Winter Garden, University of British Columbia Botanical Garden—Vancouver, British Columbia

Winter is also a prime season to visit conservatories and many Asian gardens.

REGIONAL SPECIALTY NURSERIES

Many regional specialty nurseries have display gardens, and a broad selection is provided below. Touring such specialty nursery display gardens often proves to be an education in itself; visitors can see how the plants they are buying will grow to maturity, which growing conditions are the best for their new acquisitions, and how to combine them attractively with other plants in a garden setting.

Because many specialty nurseries grow their own stock, buyers are likely to get healthy, vigorous plants well suited to local growing conditions.

Many of these nurseries are located at the proprietors' homes; please, always phone ahead for business hours and directions.

OREGON

SOUTHERN OREGON
Siskiyou Rare Plant Nursery
2825 Cummings Rd
Medford, OR 97501

(503) 772-6846
Mail orders
Visits by appointment only

The display gardens here include low-mounding rockeries, screes, and raised sand beds in which rare and hard-to-propagate alpines and rock plants are tested for their gardenworthiness. The nursery secures much of its plant material from seed exchanges and rare plant societies from around the world; its stated mission is "to bring together an ever-changing collection of the choicest dwarf plants, most under 12 inches at maturity, with the best qualities of foliage and flower." A border of native trees and some beds featuring groundcovers suitable for wild gardens are recent additions to the 4-acre nursery grounds.

Specialties: alpines, rock plants, woodland plants, dwarf conifers, hardy ferns, and dwarf Japanese maples.

CENTRAL OREGON
Cooley's Gardens
P.O. Box 126   Phone: (503) 873-5463
11553 Silverton Rd NE   Mail orders
Silverton, OR 97381

The Cooley family has been growing iris for several generations; every year they hold a festival during the peak iris viewing period (usually in the third week in May), when visitors are welcome to browse the nursery garden.

Specialty: tall bearded iris.

Gossler Farms Nursery
1200 Weaver Rd   (503) 746-3922
Springfield, OR 97478-9691   Mail orders

The ½-acre display garden combines unusual shrubs, trees, flowering perennials, and ornamental grasses. Garden tours by arrangement March–June.

Specialties: magnolias, stewartias, *Hamamelis*.

Greer Gardens
1280 Goodpasture Island Rd   (503) 686-8266
Eugene, OR 97401-1794   Mail orders

Owner Harold Greer is a noted rhododendron hybridizer, and his 13-acre nursery grounds are ablaze with the blooms of mature shrubs during April and May. Unusual varieties of Japanese maples, native plants, wildflowers, and bonsai materials also are available.

Specialties: rhododendrons, azaleas, ornamental trees.

Macleay Perennial Gardens
1420 Howell Prairie Rd SE   (503) 581-3592
Salem, OR 97301   Visits by appointment only

Retired horticulturist Robert Long has created a 3-acre nursery in the forest that features flowering perennials from around the world planted in informal beds and borders. In mid-April bleeding hearts and primroses are in full bloom; dogwoods and 10-foot-high giant lilies (*Cardiocrinum* spp.) flower in June; July visitors will see over 100 kinds of perennials at their peak.

Specialties: Japanese maples (many *palmatum* and *japonicum* varieties), *Sciadopitys verticillata, Cardiocrinum* spp.

Nichols Garden Nursery
1190 N Pacific Hwy   (503) 928-9280
Albany, OR 97321   Mail orders

The compact and attractive herb display gardens here look their best in June and July, but the real draw is the spacious old barnlike building housing Nichols's extensive selection of seeds of flower, herb, and vegetable varieties that acclimatize well to maritime Pacific Northwest growing conditions.

Specialties: herbs, gourmet vegetable seeds.

PORTLAND AND ENVIRONS
Barn Owl Nursery
22999 SW Newland Rd   (503) 638-0387
Wilsonville, OR 97070

Late June is the best time to view these handsome herb gardens, in which yew hedges and conifers serve as permanent backdrops and garden dividers. Each display area has an intriguing theme, such as silver-leaved plants, scented herbs with pink flowers, or plants found in Colonial door gardens. The nursery sponsors an annual Herb Festival during the first two weeks of May.

Specialties: herbs, perennials, scented geraniums.

The Bovees Nursery
1737 SW Coronado   (503) 244-9341
Portland, OR 97219

Rhododendrons, azaleas, and camellias bloom in the display area from February through June.

Specialties: species and hybrid rhododendrons, Japanese maples.

Caprice Farm
15425 SW Pleasant Hill Rd   (503) 625-7421
Sherwood, OR 97140   Mail orders

Several acres of test gardens overlooking spectacular views of Mount Hood bloom with peonies (May), iris (late May to mid-July), and daylilies (from early July). You may catch owner Al Rogers in the cool of the evening, moving up and down the rows of daylilies with brushes and little bags, collecting pollen for new hybrids.

Specialties: daylilies, hostas, peonies, Japanese and Siberian iris.

The Gables

21260 S Springwater Rd   (503) 631-7514

Estacada, OR 97023   Visits by appointment only, Apr–Oct

The exceptionally attractive 5-acre display areas at this nursery include a Mediterranean garden, a secret garden, a woodland garden, two rose gardens, and a tropical woods. May and early June see the roses and clematis in full bloom. Group tours by arrangement.

Specialties: unusual perennials, trees, and shrubs, many of them grown from seed.

Ingraham's Cottage Garden

370 C St, Box 126   (503) 873-8610

Scotts Mills, OR 97375   Mail orders

Climbers scramble over wooden arbors and modern hybrids edge brick paths in this rose garden adjoining a restored Victorian farmhouse. Free-ranging ducks and cooing doves add to the pleasantly rustic atmosphere.

Specialties: antique and rare roses, some hybrid teas.

Porterhowse Farms

41370 SE Thomas Rd   (503) 668-5834

Sandy, OR 97055   Mail orders

      Visits by appointment only

Displays of bonsai, *penjing,* and planted hypertufa troughs ornament the nursery grounds, which also feature a new hillside garden planted in alpines, rock plants, and flowering perennials.

Specialties: dwarf and unusual conifers, bonsai, rock plants.

Swan Island Dahlias

P.O. Box 800   (503) 266-7711

995 NW 22nd St   Mail orders

Canby, OR 97013

Fifty acres of dahlias glow and smoulder in August and September, when visitors may view them daily during daylight hours. Dahlia tubers may be purchased March through mid-June.

Specialty: dahlias.

Walden West

5744 Crooked Finger Rd NE
Scotts Mills, OR 97375

(503) 873-6875
Mail orders
Visits by appointment only

Five hundred varieties of hostas grow in planting beds in a pleasant forest setting; groundcovers and perennials also are available.

Specialty: hostas.

WASHINGTON

SOUTHERN AND CENTRAL WASHINGTON

Collector's Nursery

1602 NE 162nd Ave
Vancouver, WA 98684

(206) 256-8533
Mail orders
Visits by appointment only

This nursery's exceptionally attractive display garden features over 2500 varieties of plants, many of them shade-lovers with distinctive foliage. The garden flowers most profusely from April through June. Unusual Pacific Northwest natives are propagated here, including alpines and conifers native to nearby Mount Hood and Mount Adams and to the Siskiyou Mountains in southern Oregon.

Specialties: Pacific Northwest natives; alpines; hostas; *Trycyrtis*; iris species including Pacific Coast iris; epimediums; dwarf and rare conifers.

Connell's Dahlias

10216 40th Ave E
Tacoma, WA 98446

(206) 531-0292
Mail orders

Visit the 8-acre display area in August and September, when over 500 varieties of dahlias are in bloom.

Specialty: dahlias.

Friends and Neighbors Perennial Gardens

24708 NE 152nd Ave
Battle Ground, WA 98604

(206) 687-2962

Shady borders filled with flowering perennials and lush woodland plants spread out under a forest canopy; spring and fall show maximum color.

Specialties: perennials; woodland and shade plants.

Hall Gardens

Route 1, Box 231/F   (206) 665-4753
Ocean Park, WA 98640

This sheltered 4-acre garden tucked into Long Beach Peninsula features half-tender exotics, such as Australian mountain pepper (*Tasmania lanceolata*) and Chilean lantern bush (*Crinodendron hookerianum*), some unusual species and hybrid rhododendrons, and a pond stocked with water lilies. The best time to view flowering rhodies is late April to early May. Guided tours by arrangement.

Specialties: unusual flowering trees, shrubs, perennials, and herbs, including some plants native to Australia and New Zealand.

Jackson Nursery

31805 NE George Rd   (206) 834-2555
Camas, WA 98607

Owner Horace Jackson creates trough gardens and bonsai, hybridizes rhododendrons, and propagates many varieties of maples, shade trees, and flowering trees. In an unusual shady rock garden, moss-covered basalt rocks are interplanted with epimediums, alpine lady's mantle (*Alchemilla alpina*), and a rare, unnamed form of Japanese azalea. (Watch for the topiary snake, formed from cotoneaster, that slithers across one of the rocks.)

Specialties: rock plants, grafted Japanese maples, dwarf conifers, and rhododendrons.

Lilies and More

12400 NE 42nd Ave   (206) 573-4696
Vancouver, WA 98686   Mail orders (lilies only)

Billie Mathieu's display garden features lilies interplanted with tall ornamental grasses and a lush little water-lily pond; if you visit when the lilies bloom (June to September), whole pockets of the garden seem saturated with their exquisite scent.

Specialties: Asiatic, Oriental, and aurelian lilies.

Robyn's Nest Nursery

7802 NE 63rd St   (206) 256-7399
Vancouver, WA 98662   Mail orders

About 500 varieties of hostas are on display (200 of which are available for sale), along with such companion plants as ligularias, ferns, lilies, astilbe, and iris.

Specialties: hostas and companion plants; ornamental grasses.

OLYMPIC PENINSULA
B & D Lilies

330 "P" St   (206) 385-1738
Port Townsend, WA 98368   Mail orders

At the time of writing, B & D is developing Snow Creek Nursery, a 5-acre display garden of lilies and companion plants located 20 minutes' drive from Port Townsend. When completed, the display areas will show how lilies perform in various garden environments, such as naturalistic woodlands, wetlands, and a Japanese garden. Group tours by arrangement.

Specialties: species, Oriental, and tetraploid Asiatic lilies; daylilies; astilbes; alstroemeria; hostas.

Cedarbrook Herb Farm

986 Sequim Ave S   (206) 683-7733
Sequim, WA 98382   Mail orders (gift items only)

Display areas featuring organically grown herbs surround an attractive old farmhouse that houses a small gift shop and drying rooms for flowers and herbs. Early summer finds the herb display areas at their best.

Specialties: 200 varieties of herbs, with an emphasis on ornamental, tea, and flowering varieties.

Whitney Gardens and Nursery

P.O. Box F   (206) 796-4411
Brinnon, WA 98320   Mail orders

Visit this 7-acre rhododendron nursery from March through mid-April to view early-blooming varieties; the fullest display of blooms usually occurs in the first two weeks of May. Over 2500 species or hybrids are represented. Admission to viewing area: $1. Guided tours by arrangement.

Specialties: species and hybrid rhododendrons.

SEATTLE AND ENVIRONS
A & D Peonies

6808 180th SE   (206) 668-9690;
Snohomish, WA 98290   from Seattle, 485-2487
                                        Mail orders

Single peonies bloom in mid-May; the doubles and the Japanese varieties bloom in the first two weeks of June. The peony display fields border a woodland area featuring hostas and daylilies. Guided tours by arrangement.

Specialties: herbaceous peonies, tree peonies, hybrid daylilies, hostas.

Bamboo Gardens of Washington

5016 192nd Pl NE   (206) 868-5166

Redmond, WA 98053-4602   Mail orders (bamboo artifacts only)

This nursery's unusual display areas feature dwarf, mid-sized, and timber bamboos, rock water basins, and Japanese-style fences and gates made from bamboo. The nursery also features some tubs of hardy water lilies and other water plants.

Specialties: bamboo plants; bamboo fences, gates, and deer scarers; ornamental grasses; water plants.

Barfod's Hardy Ferns

23622 Bothell Way   (206) 483-0205

Bothell, WA 98021   Mail orders

Owner Torben Barfod evaluates ferns from around the world for U.S. winter hardiness. Two of Mr. Barfod's most dramatic "finds," the 10-to-15-foot-high Tasmanian tree fern *Dicksonia antarctica* and its cousin from New Zealand, *D. fibrosa,* unfurl their fronds in a small but magical display garden composed of mossy stones, ponds, ferns, and groundcovers located next to the greenhouses.

Specialties: hardy ferns; a small selection of fern allies.

Bassetti's Crooked Arbor Gardens

18512 NE 165th   (206) 788-6767

Woodinville, WA 98072   Mail orders

A pleasant rural setting of fields and woods frames the compact rock garden planted with unusual alpines, rock plants, and dwarf conifers. Visitors can bring their lunches to enjoy under a 65-foot-long rustic arbor bordered by flowering shrubs and perennials. Guided tours by arrangement.

Specialties: dwarf conifers, alpine plants.

Cricklewood Nursery

11907 Nevers Rd   (206) 568-2829

Snohomish, WA 98290   Mail orders

This attractive cottage garden is at peak bloom in May and June; picnickers are welcome. Guided tours by arrangement.

Specialties: herbaceous border perennials; a small selection of rare rock plants and New Zealand natives.

Good Shepherd Nursery

7016 Jones Ave NW
Seattle, WA 98117

(206) 783-8262
Visits by appointment only

This urban lot is a cornucopia of edible and ornamental plants, including fruit trees and shrubs well adapted to an urban setting. The garden, grown according to organic principles, also features espaliered fruit trees and drought-tolerant borders.

Specialties: unusual and drought-tolerant perennials and grasses.

Grand Ridge Nursery

27801 SE Highpoint Way
Issaquah, WA 98027

(206) 392-1896
Visits by appointment only

The British Rock Garden Society considers Grand Ridge's the finest collection of alpines in existence, and alpine growers from around the globe visit the nursery to learn new propagating and growing techniques. Many unusual alpines and rock plants are displayed in raised beds and screes; special treasures are featured in a small but choice collection of stone troughs near the nursery entrance. The gardens are in bloom from early March through late June. Guided tours by arrangement.

Specialties: alpines; stoneware containers.

The Herbfarm

32804 Issaquah-Fall City Rd
Fall City, WA 98024

(206) 784-2222

This establishment offers herbs planted in theme display gardens, potted for sale in the nursery area, dried in wreaths and potpourris, and cooked in gourmet luncheons in an adjoining restaurant.

Specialties: 600 varieties of herbs.

Heronswood

7530 288th NE
Kingston, WA 98346

(206) 297-4172
Mail orders
Visits by appointment only

Heronswood's pleasant 1½-acre display garden includes plants native to Japan, Korea, China, Africa, New Zealand, and Tasmania that have ornamental potential for Pacific Northwest gardens.

Specialties: unusual perennials, shrubs, and trees, with an emphasis on Asiatic species.

Moorehaven Water Gardens

3006 York Rd   (206) 743-6888
Everett, WA 98204

Chris and Val Moore have designed a delightful water garden featuring a natural pond, a bog, fountains, and several large holding ponds for water lilies. With fish darting, dragonflies humming, and frogs booming, the entire nursery vibrates with fecund life. The staff answers questions on constructing, stocking, and maintaining ponds.

Specialties: hardy water lilies, lotus, and aquatic, bog, and waterside plants; ornamental fish.

MsK Rare Plant Nursery

20066 15th Ave NW   (206) 546-1281
Seattle, WA 98177   Visits by appointment only

Mareen Kruckeberg invites visitors to wander through the large display garden that borders the nursery's greenhouse. This 4-acre "arboretum," the result of over 30 years of collecting and growing unusual plants, contains 2000 varieties of native and exotic trees, shrubs, ferns, rock plants, and groundcovers.

Specialties: Northwest native plants; rare trees, shrubs, ferns, and other plants from around the world that have proved hardy to our climate.

Pat's Perennials

7531 224th St SE   (206) 483-6634
Woodinville, WA 98072

The 4-acre display gardens feature perennials, shade plants, and rock plants. The gardens generally look their most lavish in early summer. Guided tours by arrangement for a small fee.

Specialties: 800 varieties of perennials and rock plants.

Silver Bay Herb Farm

9151 Tracyton Blvd   (206) 692-1340
Bremerton, WA 98310

Winding down a gravel drive past a small barn, visitors reach several compact herb display areas—with culinary, medicinal, fragrance, and drought-tolerant themes—that give onto views of Dyes Inlet. Guided tours by arrangement for a small fee.

Specialties: 200 varieties of culinary, medicinal, and ornamental herbs; dried flowers; seeds.

Soos Creek Gardens

12602 SE Petrovitsky Rd   (206) 226-9308
Renton, WA 98058   Visits by appointment only

These 3½-acre grounds feature natural ponds and wetlands fringed by aquatics, bog plants, grasses, and natives.

Specialties: aquatic plants and natives.

Stone Hollow Farm

21302 SE 1st   (206) 391-2218
Redmond, WA 98053-7059

Stone Hollow Farm's display garden features nicely sited rocks that clamber down an embankment to a pond. Narrow stone paths weave through the rockwork, which is planted with pungent herbs, lavenders, rosemaries, and a lively mix of flowering perennials. Guided tours by arrangement.

Specialties: perennials and herbs, with an emphasis on drought-tolerant varieties.

Village Green Perennial Nursery

10223 26th Ave SW   (206) 767-7735
Seattle, WA 98146

Owners Teresa and Bob Berridge have created an extensive display garden of flowering perennials, shrubs, small ornamental trees, and groundcovers that rims two ponds and a stream and cascades down a hill. A border near the nursery driveway features old roses (climbers and ramblers) as well as hybrid teas. The garden is in bloom from April until October, with best displays in May. Guided tours by arrangement.

Specialties: hardy flowering perennials, old roses.

NORTHERN WASHINGTON
Gardens of Art and Big Rock Nursery

2900 Sylvan St   (206) 734-4167
Bellingham, WA 98226

This 2½-acre gallery/nursery—beautifully sited on a forested hillside overlooking a lake—offers over 150 varieties of Japanese maples, a full range of Robin Hill, Linwood, and North Tisbury azalea cultivars, and almost 1000 rhododendron cultivars. Sculptures, murals, Japanese-style garden bells, and other outdoor art created by noted artists are set about the grounds. Guided tours by arrangement.

Specialties: garden sculptures; unusual Japanese maples, rhododendrons, and azaleas.

Groh's Gardens

5133 Reese Hill Rd   (206) 988-2033
Sumas, WA 98295   Visits by appointment only

This herb display garden is such a stunner—waves of soft yellows, pinks, and dusty greens set off by silvery-gray free-form fences made from driftwood—that visitors will become instant converts to herb gardening, no matter what their previous horticultural interests or inclinations. Guided tours by arrangement.

Specialties: herbs, perennials.

Waverley Gardens

4321 Silvana Terrace Rd   (206) 652-0300
Stanwood, WA 98292

June is the month when this 7-acre nursery's perennial borders and rose- and wisteria-covered pergolas are at their peak of bloom. It also features a knot garden, peacock pens, and a trickling stream.

Specialties: unusual perennials and herbs, old European roses.

West Shore Acres

956 Downey Rd   (206) 466-3218
Mount Vernon, WA 98273   Mail orders

The 1½-acre display garden wraps around a fine old Victorian farmhouse built in 1886. Unusual copper beeches and various mature shrubs act as stately backdrops to the spring-flowering bulbs flooding the garden floor during March and April, the months when the garden is open to the public. Visitors can order tulip and daffodil bulbs from the office across the parking lot, which also sells bunches of fresh-cut flowers in season.

Specialties: daffodils, tulips.

Other nurseries with flowering bulb display gardens in the area include **Roozengaarde,** 1587 Beaver Marsh Rd, Mount Vernon, (206) 424-8531, open daily during daylight hours; and **Skagit Valley Gardens,** 1695 Johnson Rd, Mount Vernon, (206) 424-6760, open daily 9–6.

EASTERN WASHINGTON
Lamb Nurseries
E 101 Sharp Ave   (509) 328-7956
Spokane, WA 99202   Mail orders
The test grounds here, a big urban lot near downtown Spokane, display a cheerful mix of flowering perennials. Plants hardy to U.S. Zone 5 (-20 to 10 degrees) are emphasized.
Specialties: hardy perennials; rock plants.

BRITISH COLUMBIA

VANCOUVER AND MAINLAND
Ferncliff Gardens
8394 McTaggert St   (604) 826-2447
Mission, BC V2V 5V6   Mail orders
Ferncliff Gardens offers several compact display gardens and 6-plus acres of growing fields featuring iris, peonies, and dahlias. View blooming iris from late May until early June, peonies around June 10th, and dahlias from late August through September.
Specialties: iris, peonies, dahlias, daylilies.

Lindell Lilies
5510 239th St   (604) 534-4729
Langley, BC V3A 7N6   Mail orders
A half-acre display area features blooming Asiatic lilies in July and stately Orientals in August.
Specialties: Asiatic, trumpet, martagon, and Oriental lilies.

Lower Mainland Nurseries
23245 40th Ave, Rural Route #12   (604) 533-2681
Langley, BC V3A 7B9
Several acres displaying informal plantings of hedge plants, evergreen shrubs, and groundcovers can be visited here throughout the growing season.
Specialties: ornamental evergreen shrubs, groundcovers, and some conifers.

Rainforest Gardens
13139 224th St, Rural Route #2   (604) 467-4218
Maple Ridge, BC V2X 7E7   Mail orders
                                    Visits by appointment only
Perennial borders, a hosta border, and beds bordering a creek offer viewing

interest throughout the growing season.

Specialties: shade-loving perennials, native plants, hostas.

VANCOUVER ISLAND

Firwood Nursery

5631 Batu Rd   (604) 658-5102

Victoria, BC V8Z 6K5   Visits by appointment only

This 2-acre nursery features a forest garden of species and hybrid rhododendrons, with best viewing times running from April through May.

Specialties: species and hybrid rhododendrons.

Haida Gold Gardens

769 Chaster Rd   (604) 338-8345

Courteney, BC V9N 5P2   Visits by appointment only

A half-acre display garden surrounding the proprietors' home features some of the hybrid rhododendrons for sale at this nursery. Visit in May for maximum bloom.

Specialty: hybrid rhododendrons.

Hazelwood Farm

13576 Adshead Rd, Rural Route #1   (604) 245-8007

Ladysmith, BC V0R 2E0

The display garden has almost 300 varieties of cooking and medicinal herbs; it blooms most profusely from mid-June through August. The owners are planting more display areas, including a knot garden.

Specialty: herbs.

Hillier Water Gardens and Nursery

P.O. Box 662   (604) 752-6109

985 Howard Rd

Qualicum Beach, BC V9K 1T2

This nursery features a series of ponds surrounded by moisture-loving plants, as well as equipment and materials for installing fountains and ponds.

Specialties: floating and submerged aquatics, waterside plants, ornamental grasses, and ferns.

Millar Mountain Nursery
5086 McLay Rd, Rural Route #3   (604) 748-0487
Duncan, BC V9L 2X1   Mail orders
    The half-acre display areas include a pond, a rock wall, a shady woodland room featuring native plants, and a sunny area planted with roses and iris. Visit in May and June to view the iris; roses bloom in late June through summer.
    Specialties: species iris, hostas.

Raven Hill Herb Farm
1330 Mt. Newton Crossroad, Rural Route #2   (604) 652-4024
Saanichton, BC V0S 1M0
    A low stone wall planted in herbs leads to a stunning valley view. There are also display beds of culinary herbs and herbal groundcovers, an organic vegetable garden, and bulbs that bloom through April, May, and June.
    Specialty: culinary herbs.

PRIVATE GARDEN TOURS

Touring private gardens is not only fun, but it also shows us how fellow gardeners solve challenges of space, labor, and plant availability that often are similar to our own. Many accomplished gardeners live in the Pacific Northwest; when they generously open their gates to the public during tours, visitors can gain a world of valuable gardening ideas.

This section lists regional garden clubs, visitors' bureaus, and community associations that sponsor periodic tours of private gardens.

OREGON

Albany Visitors Association
300 W 2nd Ave   (800) 526-2256
Albany, OR 97321

Every third weekend in July, Albany holds its Summer Victorian Days festival, during which there are guided tours of some of the town's 300 or more historic homes and gardens. Contact the association for information on the tours, as well as a brochure for a year-round self-guiding tour of private homes and gardens in the downtown historic district.

Hardy Plant Society of Oregon
P.O. Box 609
Beaverton, OR 97005

The society publishes a booklet listing private gardens and specialty nurseries throughout the state that society members can visit, by advance arrangement, from early April through October. The society also sponsors study weekends, during which members tour private gardens as part of the program. Write for a membership application.

Riverdale Parent-Teacher Community Club

Riverdale School

11733 SW Breyman Ave   (503) 636-4511

Portland, OR 97219

Every other year, in even years, this organization sponsors a tour of homes and gardens in Portland's Dunthorpe neighborhood, where Elk Rock is located. The tour is open to the general public.

WASHINGTON

Arboretum Foundation

University of Washington XD-10   (206) 325-4510

Seattle, WA 98195

The foundation occasionally offers tours of regional private gardens, specialty nurseries, and public gardens to members. Call or write for membership information.

Associated Garden Clubs of Spokane

This Spokane organization sponsors a yearly garden tour usually held during the second weekend in July. Call the Spokane Department of Parks and Recreation at (509) 456-4331 for the name and telephone number of the current garden tour chairperson. The tour is open to the general public.

Bainbridge Arts Council

261 Madison Ave S, Suite 104   (206) 842-7901

Bainbridge Island, WA 98110

"Bainbridge in Bloom" is an annual tour of Bainbridge Island gardens held on the second or third weekend in July. Works of art and crafts by local artists also are available. The tour is open to the general public; advance ticket purchase is necessary.

The Center for Urban Horticulture

University of Washington GF-15   (206) 543-8616

Seattle WA 98195

The center sponsors a regular series of classes and workshops, some of which include tours of regional private gardens, specialty nurseries, and public gardens. Call or write to be placed on the mailing list for the center's newsletter.

Ikenobo Gardens

23025 NE 8th St   (206) 868-0589
Redmond, WA 98053-7230

At the time of writing, owner Patricia Swerda was offering a guided tour of this several-acre Japanese-style garden combined with lunch at a country club for $24.50.

Madrona Community Council

c/o Jill Gordon
1529 34th Ave   (206) 329-9836
Seattle, WA 98122

Seattle's Madrona neighborhood features mature gardens on roomy urban lots on its annual garden tour, usually held the last weekend in April. The tour is open to the general public.

The Northwest Horticulture Society

Isaacson Hall
University of Washington GF-15   (206) 527-1794
Seattle, WA 98195

The society occasionally offers tours of private gardens for members. Call or write for membership information.

The Northwest Perennial Alliance

P.O. Box 45574, University Station
Seattle, WA 98145-0574

The alliance sponsors four separate tours for members during the growing season. The tours usually include members' gardens in Seattle and nearby areas. Write for membership information.

Snohomish Garden Club

P.O. Box 1204
Snohomish, WA 98290

This annual tour of private gardens in Snohomish and its environs is usually held the last Sunday in July. The tour is open to the general public. Write for information.

Whatcom County in Bloom Garden Society

The Whatcom County in Bloom Garden Society and Whatcom County Parks and Recreation sponsor an annual tour of Bellingham-area gardens in early July.

The tour is open to the general public. Call Whatcom County Parks and Recreation at (206) 592-2223 for information. The tour is open to the general public.

BRITISH COLUMBIA

Victoria Conservatory of Music

839 Academy Close   (604) 386-5311
Victoria, BC V8V 2X8

This organization sponsors an annual three-day tour of private gardens in the Victoria area in early April. The tour is open to the general public.

Victoria Horticultural Society

(604) 595-4078

This society sponsors tours of private gardens for its members during spring, summer, and fall. Out-of-area visitors may phone two weeks in advance to request admittance to forthcoming tours.

GLOSSARY

alpine: a plant native to mountain terrain that lies above the tree line and below the year-round snow line.

annual: a plant that grows from seed to complete its life cycle within a year.

arboretum: a collection of woody plants developed for purposes of research and education.

botanical garden: a collection of woody and herbaceous plants developed for purposes of research and education.

cultivar: a special variant of a plant species that usually does not reproduce true from seed, but must be propagated by cuttings, division, or grafting.

deciduous: a term applied to trees and shrubs that lose their leaves during fall and winter.

estate garden: a formerly private garden, usually developed by one individual or family, that is now open to the public.

evergreen: a term applied to plants that stay in leaf year-round.

garden room: an area within a garden that forms a distinct spatial unit.

hardscapes: architectural features in the garden, such as walls, paths, terraces, and arbors.

hybrid: a plant created by crossing two distinct parent species or varieties.

parterres: a group of flower beds arranged to form a pattern and separated by paths.

perennial: a plant whose life cycle exceeds two years.

plant palette: a term used by garden designers to encompass the entire range of plants selected for a particular garden or landscape with reference to their forms, textures, and colors.

scree: an accumulation of angular rock fragments found at the base of a cliff or steep slope; often replicated in rock gardens as a habitat for alpines and rock plants.

species: a plant population that shares common attributes and usually reproduces true from seed.

topiary: a term relating to the practice of clipping plants into the shapes of birds, animals, and other objects.

INDEX

Cricklewood Nursery, 158
Crystal Springs Rhododendron Garden, 32–33, 146
Crystal Garden, 134–35, 144, 147, 148

D
Darlingtonia Botanical Wayside, 20, 146, 148
Deepwood Gardens, 24–27, 145, 148
Downtown Parks and Squares, Portland. *See* Portland Downtown Parks and Squares
Downtown Gardens, Seattle. *See* Seattle Downtown Gardens
Dr. Sun Yat-Sen Classical Chinese Garden, 111–14, 143, 148

E
Elk Rock, the Garden of the Bishop's Close, 34–36, 143, 145, 147, 148
Erna Gunther Ethnobotanical Garden, 84, 146

F
Fairhaven Rose Garden, 99, 147
Fantasy Garden World, 115, 145, 147
Ferncliff Gardens, 163
Fireman's Park, 57
Firwood Nursery, 164
Fragrance Garden. *See* Tennant Lake Nature Walk/Fragrance Garden/Hovander
   Homestead
Friends and Neighbors Perennial Gardens, 155
Froggwell Garden, 72, 145

G
Gables, The, 154
Gardens of Art and Big Rock Nursery, 161
George Owen Memorial Rose Garden, 21–22, 147
Good Shepherd Nursery, 159
Gossler Farms Nursery, 152
Government House Gardens, 135–37, 145, 146, 147
Grand Ridge Nursery, 159
Greer Gardens, 152
Groh's Gardens, 162
Grotto, The, 36–37

Q
Queen Elizabeth Park and Bloedel Conservatory,   120, 144, 145, 146, 147, 148

R
Rainforest Gardens,   163–64
Raven Hill Herb Farm,   165
Rhododendron Park,   73, 146, 148
Rhododendron Species Foundation Display Gardens,   66–68, 145, 146
Richmond Nature Park,   121, 146, 147
Robyn's Nest Nursery,   156
Roche Harbor Resort Garden,   98–99, 145
Roozengaarde,   162
Rothschild House,   71, 147

S
Seattle Downtown Gardens,   82–84
Sehome Hill Arboretum,   99–100, 143, 146
Sendall Gardens,   128–29, 145, 147
Shore Acres State Park Botanical Garden,   18–19, 144, 145, 148
Silver Bay Herb Farm,   160
Siskiyou Rare Plant Nursery,   151
Skagit Valley Gardens,   162
Sooke Harbour House Gardens,   142, 145
Soos Creek Gardens,   161
South Slough Estuarine Reserve,   20, 146
Stanley Park Rose Garden,   121–22, 147
Stone Hollow Farm,   161
Sunken Rose Garden at Peninsula Park,   48, 147
Swan Island Dahlias,   154

T
Tallina's Garden,   48, 147
Tennant Lake Nature Walk/Fragrance Garden/Hovander Homestead,   100–101, 145, 146, 147
Tilth and Good Shepherd Demonstration Gardens,   88, 145

U
University of British Columbia Botanical Garden and Nitobe Memorial Garden,   122–25, 143, 144, 146, 147, 149

GARDEN NOTES

ABOUT THE AUTHOR

Jan Kowalczewski Whitner is a contributing editor for *Greater Seattle* magazine. Her articles on garden design have appeared in *Fine Gardening, Garden Design,* and *Pacific Northwest* magazines, the *Seattle Times,* and many other regional and national publications. Her first book, *Stonescaping,* was published in 1992. Jan lives with her family in Seattle.

Alaska Northwest Books™ proudly recommends more of its books on Northwest lifestyle:

NORTHWEST LANDSCAPING: A Practical Guide to Creating the Garden You've Always Wanted, by Mike Munro.
For weekend gardeners and avid horticulturalists alike, *Northwest Landscaping* is an invaluable sourcebook for creating a new landscape or improving an existing one. Learn how to visualize and create a garden that reflects your style and meets your budget with expert advice on how to select and use the right planting and building materials. With color photographs and 50 how-to illustrations.
Softbound, 192 pages, $16.95, ISBN 0-88240-393-1

CAPRIAL'S SEASONAL KITCHEN: An Innovative Chef's Menus and Recipes for Easy Home Cooking, by Caprial Pence.
Award-winning Portland chef Caprial Pence invites the home cook to discover the secrets of her innovative cooking style. The freshest seasonal ingredients are combined in simple, yet elegant ways. Delectable menus with 116 recpies are perfect for satisfying family and friends.
Hardbound, 240 pages, $19.95, ISBN 0-88240-417-2
Softbound, 240 pages, $12.95, ISBN 0-88240-418-0

SEATTLE BREWS: The Insider's Guide to Neighborhood Alehouses, Brewpubs, and Bars, by Bart Becker.
Here at last is the definitive guide to fine handcrafted beer in Seattle, one of the world's leading gourmet beer-producing regions. This entertaining book describes 100 Seattle drinkeries, as well as offering beer history, instructions on how to store, pour, drink, and cook with beer, and more. With illustrations, 1 map.
Softbound, 180 pages, $9.95, ISBN 0-88240-425-3

SEATTLE EMERGENCY ESPRESSO: The Insider's Guide to Neighborhood Coffee Spots, by Heather Doran Barbieri.
Espresso cravers can now find more than 100 espresso carts, coffee houses, cafes, and restaurants in the Seattle area. Arranged by neighborhood, *Seattle Emergency Espresso* describes the ambiance and edibles, how to get there, and payment policies. You'll also find intriguing bits of history on the local coffee scene, recipes for coffeetime treats from some of Seattle's favorite espresso joints, an introduction to the language of espresso, and more. With illustrations, 1 map.
Softbound, 176 pages, $9.95, ISBN 0-88240-399-0

Alaska Northwest Books™
An Imprint of Graphic Arts Center Publishing Company
P.O. Box 10306
Portland, OR 97210